I0761551

NEW TREASURES OF SUMERIAN LITERATURE
"WHEN THE MOON FELL FROM THE SKY"
AND OTHER WORKS

to Ulla Kasten
retiring from the Yale Babylonian Collection
after forty-two years

and to my teacher, Erle Leichty

NEW TREASURES OF SUMERIAN LITERATURE

"WHEN THE MOON FELL FROM THE SKY" AND OTHER WORKS

by

Mark E. Cohen

CDL Press

2017

LIBRARY OF CONGRESS CATALOGING-IN-PUBLICATION DATA

Names: Cohen, Mark E. translator.
Title: New treasures of Sumerian literature : When the moon fell from the sky and other works / [translated] by Mark E. Cohen.
Description: Bethesda, Md. : CDL Press, 2017. | Includes bibliographical references and index.
Identifiers: LCCN 2017008754 | ISBN 9781934309728 (alk. paper)
Subjects: LCSH: Sumerian literature—Translations into English.
Classification: LCC PJ4083 .N49 2017 | DDC 899/.9508—dc23
LC record available at https://lccn.loc.gov/2017008754

ISBN 9781934309728

Table of Contents

PREFACE

The Yale Babylonian Collection has always been a special place for me. After receiving my degree from the Oriental Studies Department of the University of Pennsylvania in 1972, Bill Hallo invited me to Yale on a post-doctoral fellowship. During that year Bill opened up the wondrous Yale Babylonian Collection to me and encouraged me to go "hunting" in it, permitting me to publish anything that had not already been assigned. I was a kid in a candy shop. In 1974, Bill invited me back for two more years, now as Associate Curator of the Yale Babylonian Collection. Bill always referred to those early 1970s as the "golden years" at Yale, when the graduate students included Tim Doty, Ben Foster, Rene Gallery, Peter Machinist, Marcel Sigrist, Dan Snell, and Norm Yoffee. And Peter Michalowski was continually in and out working on his dissertation. It was stimulating and fun for me to be with such a wonderful group of people.

Bill and I developed a warm friendship that would last until his death in 2015. At lunch, a few months before he died, Bill told me—as he had done at least a dozen times before—that one of his fondest memories was when he and I teamed up at an American Oriental Society meeting many, many years ago to play a game of bridge. I believe that to have been Bill's "Rosebud."

When Bill retired in 2002, Ben Foster was appointed Curator of the Yale Babylonian Collection. Ben has continued to show the graciousness and generosity that Bill had shown me. And for 42 years Ulla Kasten "ruled" the Yale Babylonian Collection, first as administrator and then as Associate Curator. A few years ago Ulla reminded me that I, as well as Bill, had interviewed her for the job back in 1974 and that on the day before she was to report for her new position Jack Finkelstein died—quite a way to start. Ulla retired last year and it is hard for me to imagine the Yale Babylonian Collection without her. She helped me so many times in so many ways. And whenever I came to

New Haven to work in the Collection, Ulla offered me her home and her unparalleled hospitality, as she did for so many others who visited the Collection. Lunch at Ulla's table at Yorkside Pizza was standard routine if you were visiting the Collection. Fortunately, Yale has hired Agnete Lassen as the new Associate Curator, who is continuing to make all who come to work at the Collection feel welcome.

This book includes editions of eight new Sumerian literary compositions from the Yale Babylonian Collection. I thank Ben, Ulla, and Agnete for granting me permission to publish these wonderful texts. For me, the northwest corner on the third floor of Sterling Memorial Library will always be home.

In addition, this book has an edition of one text from the private London collection of Mr. Ahmad Saeedi. It is the complete Old Babylonian recension of "Ninisina's Journey to Nippur," otherwise partially preserved in two Middle Assyrian bilingual texts and a very small fragment of an Old Babylonian text. I thank Mr. Saeedi for allowing me to publish this treasure from his collection and I also thank David Owen, who made me aware of the tablet and spoke to Mr. Saeedi on my behalf.

All nine Sumerian compositions in this book are written in Emegir, none in Emesal, although a couple Emesal terms do occur. Composition no. 1 "An Isin Investiture" is partially syllabic and no. 9 "Tears of a Fallen King" is almost entirely syllabic. Based on internal evidence, I suggest that these two texts were written by novice scribes who, up to this point, had learned the basic signs—mainly, the most common signs of the form vC or Cv—but only a handful of the more advanced signs. I believe these two texts to be the result of an exercise to test the novice scribe's mastery of those basic signs, as well as to train him to write from dictation and to hone his "penmanship." In this early stage of his scribal education, the young student was expected to use the basic signs he had just learned to phonetically represent the as-yet unlearned, less common signs when writing down a dictated Sumerian composition.

An indication of the beginning level of the scribe of syllabic text no. 9 is his inability to know when to use the correct sign to differentiate the phonemes /ĝ/ and /g/. This failing is seen in his writing ge-en (9: 10, 11) instead of ĝe$_6$-en for ĝen "to go"; saĝ-gi-ga (9:13) instead of saĝ-ĝi$_6$-ga; and gi-ĝìr (9:8) instead of gi-gir for gigir "chariot." The scribe had assuredly learned basic signs with the phonemes /g/ and /ĝ/, but apparently did not yet know when to apply them correctly.

Further, the scribe of text no. 9 was apparently unfamiliar with one standard Old Babylonian Sumerian scribal practice, folding long lines onto the same side of the tablet. The scribe of text no. 9, however, continued each line far onto the reverse. Perhaps too he felt so harried trying to keep up with the dictation that he just kept on writing.

In partially syllabic text no. 1 the scribe uses the sign YA, writing /CiyaCa/ instead of /CiaCa/, which occurs in line 18': di-ya-ba; line 24': lugal-an-ki-ya-ka; and line 26': e-ri-ya-na. Only a novice scribe would have done this. So too, the scribe of text no. 1 knew the sign nun "prince" but did not know nùn "battle," for he writes nu-un for nùn in the same line (1:10') in which he writes the NUN-sign, apparently realizing that the NUN-sign was not correct in the second case. So, not knowing the correct sign, he wrote it syllabically. Again an indication of the scribe's inexperience. Another indication that our scribe was a beginner is the writing ki-úr (1:23') for ki-ùr, hardly a mistake expected of an accomplished scribe (though such mistakes do occur). So too the writing ḫu-ur-gu-ug (1:15')—we believe for ḫul-gig—seems to indicate that the scribe didn't understand what he was hearing and writing.

Interestingly two more advanced signs he uses, piriĝ and umbin, occur in the same verse. This is part of a commonly occurring phrase and perhaps our novice scribe had come across it before, which might explain his writing these non-syllabic signs. In fact, this is the kind of expression that might have been written, for example, on a lenticular student tablet, perhaps the next stage after learning the basic, mainly monosyllabic signs. As for those who would argue that these syllabic texts were created to facilitate a scribe's reading aloud of the text by having a syllabic version in front of him, it is hard to believe that our scribe would have kept the less common, bi-syllabic sign UMBIN were that his purpose.

I am not here making a blanket statement that all syllabic Sumerian texts were written by novice scribes from dictation. However, any attempt to discover the reason or reasons behind the writing of syllabic texts in general should take our two texts into consideration.

A note on the transliteration. No matter what transliteration system one uses, we assuredly will never be able to accurately reflect how spoken Sumerian sounded. Not only are we unsure of sign pronunciation, the inclusion or omission of final consonants, and so forth, but the pronunciation of Sumerian assuredly varied from place to place and from time to time, as is true of all languages. On the other hand, we do try to achieve some semblance of how the signs may have sounded. Otherwise, we would transcribe each Sumerian text using just the sign numbers in R. Borger's *Mesopotamische Zeichenlexikon*. Until all those transcribing Sumerian texts agree to and adhere to one particular transliteration methodology, it behooves each of us to use a system that easily conveys the sign and text to the reader. I must confess that when using the ePSD in concert with the ETCSL I occasionally had difficulty in this regard. I hope no one finds such difficulty here. I still use the "old" accent and grave system when transliterating monosyllabic values, not because it is methodologically superior to the use of a subscripted sign number, but because it is consistent with standard Akkadian transliteration. Nonetheless, I do use the sign number for all multi-syllabic signs, since sometimes there has been confusion as to the vowel over which to place the marker.

I have taken the liberty of making one innovation in my transcription. Perhaps others will find it useful. I have enclosed "frozen" glosses within braces, using a smaller font size. A frozen gloss is a gloss that over time, because of its continued use, became part of the standardized writing of the term itself and was written on the line and in the same size as the term being elucidated (see B. Jagersma, *A Descriptive Grammar of Sumerian*, p. 19). Thus, for example, the writing ULU_3.LU "storm" is transcribed here as ulu_3{lu} rather than, as is now frequently done, u_{18}-lu, which, I believe, misrepresents how the scribes understood the two signs. A transcription ulu_3^{lu} is also unacceptable since it would indicate a raised gloss on the tablet, which is not the case here.

Whenever in the commentary I quote a line from a Sumerian composition without citing the place of publication, the line is cited from the composite text in the Electronic Text Corpus of Sumerian Literature (ETCSL). Let me add a special thanks to those who maintain the ETCSL. It is an extremely important tool and has greatly facilitated my work.

This book contains photographs, but not copies, of each tablet, with the exception of text no. 3, NBC 5452. A copy by Nicole Brisch of that text will appear as YOS 22, no. 23 (pls. XXXII–XXXIII). I have included photographic enlargement of sections of the tablets to facilitate their reading. I thank the Yale Babylonian Collection for providing me with the photographs of their tablets and David Owen for the photographs of Mr. Saeedi's tablet. To be quite frank, I feel I no longer have—if I ever did—the ability to produce first-rate tablet copies. Moreover, in this world of digital photography, innovative techniques, and software such as Photoshop, the added value of copies is quite questionable. However, I freely admit that a beautiful, accurate tablet drawing can be a work of art and I admire those who can produce such work.

Lastly, let me say that I have absolutely, thoroughly enjoyed working on these texts, no matter how frustrating it may have been at times. Being the first person in 4,000 years to read a particular work of literature is an unrivaled experience available only to a few. I understand the excitement and the passion that I first saw in Dr. Kramer's eyes, when, as an undergraduate student at Penn's Wharton School of Business, I happened to take an elective course called "The Sumerians."

Mark E. Cohen
April 2017

Acknowledgments

If this book has credibility, it is in large part due to the efforts of my friend Antoine Cavigneaux, who meticulously checked every line of my transliteration against the photographs of the text. This painstaking and exacting work led him to propose new readings and to offer suggestions for the understanding of passages. I dread to think what this work would have looked like had I not been fortunate enough to have had the benefit of Antoine's scholarship. I told Antoine that I planned to credit his ideas in the commentary and that I also wanted to recognize his contribution on the title page. But Antoine, with his usual humility, asked that I not do so, saying that a simple recognition in the Acknowledgments would suffice. So here it is, Antoine. Thank you.

I also thank Andrew George for his comments on text no. 6, "When the Moon Fell from the Sky."

And again, I want to thank Benjamin Foster, Curator of the Yale Babylonian Collection, and Ulla Kasten and Agnete Lassen, the former and present associate curators of the Yale Babylonian Collection, for permission to publish tablets under their care, and Mr. Ahmad Saeedi for permission to publish the tablet from his collection. I also thank David Owen for the photographs of Mr. Saeedi's tablet.

ABBREVIATIONS

Abbreviations not listed below are according to *The Assyrian Dictionary of the Oriental Institute of the University of Chicago. U and W* (vol. 20) or *The Sumerian Dictionary of the University of Pennsylvania. B* (vol. 2).

Akkadische Syllabar	W. von Soden and W. Röllig, *Das Akkadische Syllabar*. Rome, 1967.
Alster, *Proverbs*	B. Alster, *Proverbs of Ancient Sumer. The World's Earliest Proverb Collections*. Bethesda, 1997.
Civil, Beer Goddess	M. Civil, "A Hymn to the Beer Goddess and a Drinking Song." *Studies Presented to A. Leo Oppenheim*. Chicago, 1964. Pp. 67–89.
Cohen, *Festivals*	M.E. Cohen, *Festivals and Calendars of the Ancient Near East*. Bethesda, 2015.
CUSAS	Cornell University Studies in Sumerology and Assyriology
ePSD	online, Pennsylvania Sumerian Dictionary Project
ETCSL	online, Electronic Text Corpus of Sumerian Literature
Litke, *A Reconstruction*	R. Litke, *A Reconstruction of the Assyro-Babylonian God-Lists, AN: ^{d}A-nu-um and AN: anu šá amēli*. New Haven, 1988.
Owen, *Irisagrig*	D. I. Owen, *Cuneiform Texts Primarily from Iri-saĝrig / Āl-Šarrākī and the History of the Ur III Period*. Nisaba 15. Bethesda, 2013.

PSD	*The Sumerian Dictionary of the University of Pennsylvania*
Rochberg, *Heavenly Writing*	F. Rochberg, *The Heavenly Writing. Divination, Horoscopy, and Astronomy in Mesopotamian Culture.* New York and Cambridge, 2004.
Sjöberg, *Mondgott*	Å.W. Sjöberg, *Der Mondgott Nanna-Suen in der sumerischen Überlieferung*. Uppsala, 1960.

1. An Isin Investiture

This work may be an "investiture" of the god Damu, the son of Ninisina, the chief goddess of Isin, though we cannot exclude the possibility that the composition is a hymn for a king of Isin.

That this work involves an investiture seems evident from lines 31'–33':

31'. An, king of the gods, the holy, august dais, the ar[tfully(?) crafted(?)] throne,
32'. ... the glistening-lapis lazuli scepter
33'. ... into its keeping ...

Moreover, in the proceeding lines Enki, Enlil, Ninisina, and Ištaran are all involved in honoring the entity.

That Damu, a major deity of Isin, is the one being honored may be deduced in line 28': (Ninisina) has named you "Damu, The-Handsome-One." Another feature suggests a deity rather than a king as the subject. Our composition concludes in broken lines 36' and 37' with the word ga-i-i "I shall praise." To our knowledge, this exact phrasing is otherwise attested only when addressing a god (see ETCSL), never a king. Lastly, the subject seems to be called šul-á-zi-da, an epithet otherwise attested only for deities (see commentary to lime 25').

However, we could translate lines 27'–28':

27'. At the Egalmaḫ of Ninisina
28'. Damu, The-Handsome-One, has called you by name.

If so, this would indicate that Damu, rather than being the one honored, is honoring someone else, presumably the king of Isin. And note that the sign LUGAL appears in a broken context in line 4.

Unfortunately the obverse is destroyed. The beginning of the reverse refers apparently to an historical event, to a military victory, perhaps the recapture of the city of Umma by the dynasty of Isin. This military success may well be a key reason the entity is being honored, this victory credited either to the god Damu or to the king of Isin.

It would appear that the battle referred to in lines 9'ff. was intended to recover territory lost either through rebellion or invasion. In line 13', the hymn refers to a great city returning: e-ri-mah-bi šu-ba im-mi-in-gi$_4$. That "great city," the one recaptured, may well have been Umma, since Ninsiĝar is mentioned in line 11'. Ninsiĝar is a goddess otherwise attested only at Ur III Umma.

Lines 29'–30' mention Ninḫursaĝ, her temple at Keš, and the temple of Ištaran. Keš's literary position in our text may indicate that during the Isin-period it had attained a position of political or religious prominence perhaps second to only Isin itself. This hypothesis is supported by the hymns of the Isin king Lipit-Ištar, in whose hymns A and B Keš is listed among the most prominent cities of Sumer, they being Nippur, Ur, Uruk, and Eridu; obviously Isin; and Keš. The temple of Ištaran in Dēr was the Edimgalkalama, but whether that is what is referenced here is unclear. Nonetheless, this reference to the cult of Ištaran would seem to show its importance during that period.

Our text is in poor condition, with much broken away, including almost the entire obverse. The text is partially syllabic. An unusual orthographic feature of the text is the scribe's use of the sign YA, writing /CiyaCa/ instead of /CiaCa/, which occurs in line 18': di-ya-ba; line 24': lugal-an-ki-ya-ka; and line 26': e-ri-ya-na. We have suggested in the preface that some syllabic texts such as this may have been the product of novice scribes. No accomplished scribe would write YA, as was done here.

YBC 7072

112×81×30

obv.

1. [x (x)]-saĝ-ĝá-maḫ ⸢an-e?⸣ [x x]-l[a? ...]
2. [...] ⸢x x x x x⸣ ⸢mu?-na?-ab?-x(-x)⸣ [...]
3. [...] ki? ⸢x⸣ [...]
4. [...] ⸢x⸣-da lugal [...]
5. [...] x x [...]
6. [...] x [...]

all but last lines completely destroyed

7'. [...] ⸢x x⸣ [...]

8'. [...] ⸢x x x x x⸣ [...]

rev.

9'. [x x (x)] e-ri(-)ir-ta gal-gal-la

10'. [x nu]n-zi-da nu-un la-bi zi-g[e$^{?}$]

11'. [(x) k]ù$^{?}$ Nin-si-ĝar e-ni(-)ir-ta mè-ḫuš ak

12'. [x] e-ri ku-ku za-ra mu-ra-an-kù

13'. [x x]-ta-ka-ka e-ri-maḫ-bi šu-ba im-mi-in-⸢gi$_{4}$⸣

14'. [x]-gal zi-zi-ge e-ri gi$_{4}$-gi$_{4}$ ta-ta

15'. [x]-ga ga-ba-ri gi lú ḫu-ur-gu-ug dab$_{5}$-d[ab$_{5}^{?}$]

16'. [x i]gi-piriĝ-ĝá ⸢umbin⸣-u$_{11}$-ri-na

17'. [x š]eg$_{11}^{?}$ gi$_{4}$-gi$_{4}$ mùš$^{?}$-bi ḫu-lu-a-ba

18'. [x d]i$^{?}$-di$^{?}$-ya-ba ur-saĝ in tar-re

19'. [x x]-a mar-za šà-ḫu-<ul$^{?}$>-ta

20'. [x x] ⸢ZU.AB⸣ ḫé-du$_{7}$-Eridu^{ki}-ga

21'. [x x ḫ]é-⸢du$_{7}$⸣-e um-mi-in-si ḫé-si-ki-le-e

22'. [x x (x)] šu-zu-šè šu mu-uš-⸢ĝál$^{?}$⸣

23'. [x x k]i-úr èš-maḫ-kur-ra-ka

24'. [x (x) k]i$^{?}$ lugal-an-ki-ya-ka

25'. [x s]u-la-zi-da mu-ši mu-ri-in-ši

26'. ì-si-in e-ri-ya-na ki-ĝar-ra kù ^{d}Nin-si-in-na i du$_{11}$-ga-re

27'. é-gal-maḫ-^{d}Nin-si-in-na-ke$_{4}$

28'. $^{d!}$Da-mu lú-sa$_{6}$-ga mu-ši mu-ri-<in>-ši

29'. ⸢ke⸣-e-sa-^{d}Nin-ḫur-saĝ-ĝá-ke$_{4}$

30'. é-Ištaran-⸢na⸣ igi-su-bi mu-ši <mu>-ri-in-ši

31'. ⸢an⸣ lugal-diĝir-re-e-ne-ke$_{4}$ bara$_{2}$-maḫ-si-ik-la-ka gu-za-ga-l[a$^{?}$-ma$^{?}$]

32'. [x x] ⸢x⸣ ^{ĝeš}ĝidri-za-gìn-⸢duru$_{5}$⸣

33'. [x x x] ⸢x⸣ šu-ba šu mu-uš-[ĝál$^{?}$]

34'. [...] ⸢lugal⸣-šùd$^{?}$-⸢dè$^{?}$⸣

35'. [...] ⸢gù mu⸣-un-ni-ib-d[é]

36'. [...-d]a$^{?}$-ar$^{?}$ ga-i-[i]

37'. [...] ⸢da$^{?}$-ar$^{?}$⸣ ga-⸢i⸣-[i]

TRANSLATION

obverse too fragmentary or destroyed

9'. ... city(?)/cities(?) being great,
10'. ... true prince who engages in ferocious battle,
11'. [ho]ly(?) (...) Ninsiĝar ... waging furious battle,
12'. ... entering(?) the city sanctified it for you.
13'. Of the abandoned(?) ... its great city has he(?) restored.
14'. Mustering(?) a great ..., turning the city back over and abandoning (it).
15'. … turning back the opponent, capturing the hostile ones.
16'. (With) the face of a lion and the talons of an eagle,
17'. roaring(?), ruining their land(?),
18'. ... inquires after the hero,
19'. ... the rites joyously(?),
20'. [may … of] the abzu, the ornament of Eridu,
21'. after fulfilling(?) the proper acts(?), purify it.
22'. ... placed(?) into your keeping.
23'. ... in the Ki'ur, the great shrine of the land,
24'. ... [the pla]ce(?) of the king of heaven and earth,
25'. has he named you "Young Man, the Right Arm."
26'. In Isin, her city, the well-founded place, after holy Ninisina has said "Hooray!"
27'. at the Egalmaḫ of Ninisina
28'. she has named you "Damu, The-Handsome-One."
29'. At the <E>Keš of Ninḫursaĝ (and)
30'. the house of Ištaran, the bright-eyed one, has she named you.
31'. An, king of the gods, the holy, august dais, the ar[tfully(?) crafted(?)] throne,
32'. … the glistening-lapis lazuli scepter
33'. … into its keeping …
34'. ... Lugalšudde(?)
35'. ... utter.
36'. ... forever(?) shall I praise!
37'. ... forever(?) shall I praise!

NOTES

9'. The meaning of e-ri(-)ir-ta is unclear. There are several possibilities. First, this term may parallel e-ni(-)ir-ta in line 11', which, if so, would suggest "city" and "her (Ninsiĝar's) house" respectively. The orthography e-ri for "city" occurs in lines 13', 14', and 26'. In light of the form gal-gal-la, perhaps e-ri-ir is for eri eri "cities." However, elsewhere (ll. 27' and 30') the scribe uses the expected é sign, which lessens the possibility that he used e for é in line 11'. If a separate term, ir-ta might be for ér-ta "amidst wailing" or ir-ta "from (the city) being pillaged." In either case we would expect ér-ra-ta or ir-ra-ta, though the possibility that our syllabic text was written by a novice scribe might account for this omission. Moreover, in line 11' we could understand e-ni-ir-ta as an orthography for a-nir-ta, "amidst lamentation" (cf. the lamentation ^{d}Utu-gin$_{7}$ è-ta, line a+219 [Cohen, *Lamentations*, I, 104]: gala-e a-še-er-ta[var. -ra] ba-ta-è *kalû ina tānīḫi itta*[*ṣi*] "the *gala*-priest left amidst lamenting"), which could suggest an interpretation of e-ri-ir-ta as being for ér-ér(-ra)-ta.

10'. There seems to be intentional word play in line 10' between the homonymous nun-zi-da and nu-un zi-ge. nun-zi would presumably refer to either Damu or the king of Isin.

We have interpreted nu-un la-bi zi-g[e$^{?}$] as syllabic for nùn lab zi-ge "to engage in ferocious battle." We do not expect nu-un here to be syllabic for nun "prince," since the scribe has already written the NUN sign at the beginning of the line and, therefore, would seem to have no reason to then write the term syllabically in the very same line. Thus nu-un should render another sign, one with which the scribe was unfamiliar, having the value /nun/, for which we suggest nùn(BU) *anantu* "battle," a rather uncommon value a novice scribe might easily not know. la-bi is attested only as a term of endearment (see ePSD), a meaning that clearly makes no sense in our context. However, keeping in mind the syllabic nature of our text, note Ea IV 307 (MSL XIV p. 367):

la-ab KAL MIN(=gu-ru-šú) *šá* UR.KAL *la-ab-bu*

indicating that the KAL sign read /lab/ conveys the ferociousness of a lion, apparently deriving from Akkadian *labbu* "ferocious." Understanding la-bi in our passage as syllabic for lab "ferocious" makes sense, for nu-un-la-bi would then parallel mè-ḫuš in the next line.

The verb zi can mean *tebû* "to attack," "to rebel."

11'. As noted above, Ninsiĝar was a goddess at Umma in the Ur III period. We know nothing of her worship in the Old Babylonian period. To our knowledge, she is absent from all extant Sumerian literary and historical texts from all periods, so her mention here is unexpected. In the Ur III period at Umma the deity had an *išib* priest (BPOA 1 1252). Ninsiĝar also had the forms—either in Umma or in villages in its environs Nin-si-ĝar-eden-na and Nin-si-ĝar-an-na (see Emesal Vocabulary I 87 [MSL IV p. 9] for the Emesal form Gašan-si-mar-an-n[a]). The form Nin-si-ĝar-an-na continued in tradition through to the first-millennium BCE god-list AN : *Anum*, IV 74, in which she is identified as a lyre of Inana (Litke, *A Reconstruction*, p. 154). We know that the cultic (and political) importance of deities waxed and waned (or entirely disappeared) from one historical period to the next. At Umma in the Sargonic period Ninilduma was apparently the major deity, but was displaced in the Ur III period by Šara. Could Ninsiĝar, in turn, have displaced Šara in the Old Babylonian period and thus symbolized Umma as perhaps in our text?

For e-ni ir-ta see out commentary to line 9' above.

The expression mè ḫuš occurs in Šulgi D 251: mè ḫuš gal "great and terrible battle" and Angim III 40 and IV 15 with translation *tāḫazi ezzi* (CAD T 42 *s.v. tāḫazu*). We have found no other references to mè ak "to wage war." However, this may reflect Akkadian influence, since the expression *tāḫaza epēšu* "to wage war" is quite common (CAD E 220 *s.v. epēšu*).

12'. For another instance of the syllabic orthography e-ri "city," see syllabic Nanna M, line 2: e-ri ab-ba-ge-en ni-ba ri-a-ta "In the city that inspires awe like the sea." The verbal forms mu-ra-ab-kù-ga and mu ra-an-kù-kù-ga occur referring to rites (šu-luḫ-ḫa, ĝarza), the heavens, and structures (see ETCSL).

13'. Another reference to maḫ used with eri "city" is "Ninurta's Journey to Eridu," line 8: eri-zu maḫ-àm é-zu maḫ-àm "Your city is great; your house is great." eri-maḫ indicates that the restored city was a major location, not just some small town overrun by an invading force.

For šu-ba gi$_4$ referring to restoration involving a city, as we suggest here, cf. Ur-Namma C, line 86: urim$_5^{ki}$ šu-ba im-mi-gi$_4$. For šu-a gi$_4$ in Old Akkadian economic texts referring to the handing over of finished products, note, e.g., CUSAS 35 187: obv. i 2.

14'. We have understood ta-ta as an orthography for da_{13}(TAK_4)-da_{13} "to abandon," indicating that the enemy troops were forced to abandon the city. It is unclear whether [...]-gal zi-zi-ge refers to the mustering of the large Isin forces, thereby causing the enemy to turn the city back over and leave, or whether it refers to the large enemy force itself getting up and leaving.

15'. Presumably ḫu-ur-gu-ug is for ḫul-gig "hostile." For lú-ḫul-gig *zêru*, see ePSD *s.v.* hulu gig.

16'. For this imagery cf. "Debate Between Bird and Fish," line 110: u_4-bi-a mušen igi pirĝ-ĝá umbin u_{11}-rí-in^{mušen}-na. An alternate form of this imagery of lion and eagle is "Gilgameš and Ḫuwawa," lines 37 and 59: šu pirĝ-ĝá umbin u_{11}-rí-in^{mušen}-na. The imagery in our passage presumably refers to either Damu, the king of Isin, or the Isin troops.

18'. in tar-re is syllabic for èn tar-re.

20'. ḫé-du_7 Eridu^{ki}-ga is Enki. Cf. "Enki and the World Order," line 42: en an-né ki-áĝ ḫé-du_7 Eridu^{ki}-ga "the lord, the beloved of An, the ornament of Eridu."

21'. It is unclear whether -e in ḫé-du_7-e is the ergative (perhaps then referring to Enki in the preceding line) or the directive ("what is proper," referring perhaps to ritual acts). For the verb si governing the directive, note Ur-Namma C, line 13: lugal ... kisal-maḫ-e si-a "the king ... occupies the august courtyard."

23'–24'. The writing ki-úr by our novice scribe is presumably for ki-ùr. Lugal-an-ki-a is an epithet of Enlil, Nanna, and Utu (see ETCSL), but, because of the reference to the ki-ùr, it refers here to Enlil.

25'. su-la-zi-da may be for šul á-zi-da. Note šul-á-zi-da, one of the seven children of Nin-Girida (Litke, *A Reconstruction*, p. 191); Ninĝišzida A, line 19: en diĝir šul á-zi-da; and Nanše A, line 29: ^{d}Nanše šul á-zi-da tuku-ni im-ma-ni-in-$saĝ_5$-e "Nanše chooses a young man of means."

mu-ši mu-ri-in-ši is for mu-šè mu-ri-in-$še_{21}$(SA_4) "to call the name." Cf. Asarluḫi A, line 9 and Šulgi P, line 39: mu-šè mu-rí-in-$še_{21}$.

26'. Another possibility is i(-i) du_{11} "to utter praise" (CAD N/1 102 for i and ii), although a form i(-i)—du_{11} is unattested.

29'. Noting the parallelism of lines 29'–30' with 27'–28', we suggest that line 29' begins with the name of Ninḫursaĝ's temple, the é-kèš^{ki}, just as line 27' begins with the name of Ninisina's temple. Our scribe seems to have omitted the initial é sign.

30'. For a thorough discussion of Ištaran and Ištaran-igi-šuba, see Sjöberg, *Temple Hymns*, pp. 130–32.

We would have expected our scribe to write šu- instead of su- for šuba, as occurs elsewhere (šu ba, ša bi [see CAD Š/3 185 *s.v. šubû* A]).

The temple of Ištaran in Dēr was the Edimgalkalama.

31'. As revealed in line 21', the scribe did not know the SIKIL sign and so wrote the value syllabically.

The term following gu-za must be descriptive of the throne, since the other objects in this passage associated with rule have descriptors. So too, the term here must be syllabic. The scribe knows how to write the GAL sign (ll. 9', 27'), so here it should be some other word beginning with /ga/, one whose sign the scribe was unfamiliar with. The only such term beginning with /ga/ we are aware of that might be appropriate here is GALAM (clearly not a basic sign), and one can see the possible beginning of a LA sign before the break.

32'. For za-gìn $duru_5$ as possibly wet-looking or a glaze, see CAD Z 11 *s.v. zagindurû*. Note that Šamaš is described as holding a lapis lazuli scepter in *RA* 38 87:12 (CAD U 200 *s.v. uqnû*): *našiātima šibirram ša uqnîm ina aḫika* "you (Šamaš) carry a scepter of lapis lazuli at your side."

34'. Lugal-šùd-dè/Umun-šùd-dè is a deity sometimes identified with Damu/Dumuzi (see, e.g., Cohen, *Lamentations*, II, 683, line 7). However, the large space between the signs LUGAL and ŠÙD suggests it might not be a proper name, but should be taken literally.

YBC 7072 obverse

YBC 7072 reverse

2. A Hymn to the Twin God(s) Enki Niraḫ for King Gungunum

Most striking in this hymn for King Gungunum of Larsa is the close pairing of the snake-deity Niraḫ with Enki, although the two are associated elsewhere. It would be natural that a cosmic serpent, Niraḫ, would dwell in the abzu, the subterranean waters, and thereby be associated with the lord of these waters, Enki. For this relationship note Gudea Cyl. A xxvii, 1: ᵈNiraḫ kù abzu dar-a-àm "Holy Niraḫ parting the abzu" and "Enki's Journey to Nippur," line 86: ĝešgi-muš-an-na ní-laḫ$_5$-a-ni (var. ᵈNiraḫ) "His (Enki's) punting pole, his rudder (var. homonym Niraḫ)." These passages indicate that the cosmic snake, Niraḫ, was associated with Enki for travel through the abzu, like an oar or rudder. For a thorough analysis of Niraḫ, see F.A.M. Wiggerman's discussion in *RlA* 9 (1998), pp. 570-74.

It is, therefore, surprising that in our composition the two are not only called "twins" (maš-tab-ba, dumu-tab-ba), but their identities seem to be intertwined. Note that the order of the names in the first two lines is reversed, indicating perhaps that the two gods are equal or even that the two gods are actually two facets of the same deity. So too the poet alternates his address between Enki and Niraḫ, as if addressing two aspects of the same deity. However, in some passages of our text the poet is clearly referring to two distinct deities. The first lines state that Enki and Niraḫ are twins; line 3 uses min-na-ne-ne "the two of them"; and line 18 uses the plural šu-ne-ne. However, line 9, which obviously alludes only to a snake, and thus to Niraḫ not Enki, names both of them: "Enki-Niraḫ, (your) major presence in the reeds is a serious matter (for) no one can find or see (you)."

Thus, we conjecture that this hymn is directed to one deity, called Enki-Niraḫ, who, at some point, formed from two separate but associated deities, Enki and Niraḫ, the latter originally seen as subservient to Enki. The dual nature of this "unified" god is made clear in line 3: (Of) the two of them, (one) was said to be "Respected" (=Niraḫ); (the other) was stated to be "Creating" (=Enki).

The closing section of the hymn with an exhortation to Enki-Niraḫ is unique. zà-mí is a standard hymnic closing and zà-mí du$_{11}$-ga might be a logical extension. But zà-mí mí-du$_{11}$-ga is unexpected, and especially e-ne-di, which denotes game-playing, mirth, and in tone highly unexpected here. There then follow two wishes. The first is that Enki-Niraḫ control the snakes. Is this a reaction to an unusual problem of snakes in some parts of the kingdom or even ophidiophobia, a fear of snakes by Gungunum? Or, perhaps there was a project of some type undertaken, such as canal work, and this hymn was part of the ritual to remove or keep snakes away. We can only speculate. The second wish has an unusual aspect. It contains a standard grant of wisdom, but, instead of granting it directly to the king, Gungunum, it grants it to the "(something) of Gungunum."

The structure of the hymn is as follows:

1-3. The dual aspect of the god-pair Enki-Niraḫ.
4-9. Enki and Niraḫ are addressed. This includes their attributes, the wisdom of the Enki aspect and the snake-like qualities of the Niraḫ aspect.
10-16. Our understanding of these lines is somewhat tentative due to the switch to the third person. Apparently good things are granted to Gungunum.
17-19. Closing exhortation to Enki-Niraḫ and wishes.

NBC 7806

104×63×33

1. ^{d}Niraḫ ^{d}En-ki ⸢maš-tab-ba-àm dumu$^{?}$-tab$^{?}$-ba$^{?}$-àm$^{?}$⸣
2. ^{d}En-ki ^{d}Niraḫ maš-tab-ba dumu-tab-ba ⸢x x⸣ mu-ni-in-i
3. min-na-ne-ne nir-ĝál ša-an-du$_{11}$ mud-dè ša-an-e
4. an-ki-šè maḫ ⸢dib-bé⸣-éš è
5. kur ki-sud-rá-šè niĝin$_{2}$-na-bi saĝ èn-tar-bi-me-en zi-ĝál-kalam-ma-me-en
6. diĝir-diĝir-ra diri-ga en gal-zu níĝ-nam-me-en gaba-ri nu-tuku-me-en
7. ^{d}En-ki dumu-an-gal-la en gal-zu níĝ-nam-me-en šà-zu níĝ ù-tu
8. ^{d}Niraḫ diĝir-lipiš gi-a gub-bé níĝ maḫ-àm nu-pà-da igi nu-bar-re
9. ^{d}En-ki ^{d}Niraḫ maḫ-bi gi-a gub-bé níĝ maḫ-àm na-pà-da igi nu-bar-re
10. lú-ulu$_{3}$-bi ĝeštug ĝar-ra ⸢saĝ$^{?}$⸣ mu-ni-in-íl ⸢umuš$^{?}$⸣ mu-ni-in-ĝar
11. kalam-ma mu še$_{21}$-ni maḫ in-ĝar
12. saĝ-ĝi$_{6}$ zi-ĝál a-na lu-a ú-saĝ a-du$_{11}$-bi e-ne-ra mu-un-ne-ĝál

13. gudug zi-diĝir-ra lú bí-in-du$_{11}$-ga níĝ-sa$_6$-ga šà-ga ru-a-ni
14. e-ne-er mu-un-na-an-ne-ĝál
15. diĝir-re-e-ne ur-maḫ piriĝ ušumgal
16. níĝ-sa$_6$-ga-a-ni mu-un-<ne$^{?}$>-ĝál
17. zà-mí mí-du$_{11}$-ga e-ne-di
18. ^{d}En-ki ^{d}Niraḫ a-na muš šu ne-ne ḫé-en-ĝál
19. ^{d}En-ki ^{d}Niraḫ ⸢x⸣ Gu-un-gu-nu-um-ma {ĝeš.túg}ĝeštug-daĝal e-ne-ra šúm-mu-na-ab

TRANSLATION

1. Niraḫ-Enki is a set of twins, is a set of twin sons.
2. Enki and Niraḫ came out … as twins, twin sons.
3. (Of) the two of them, (one) is said to be "Respected"; (the other) is stated to be "Creating."
4. Proceeding grandly through heaven and earth,
5. for far-away countries, everywhere, are you their caretaker; you are the life(-giving force) of the nation.
6. Among the gods surpassing, you are the lord wise in all matters; you have no rival.
7. Enki, child of great An, you are the lord wise in all matters, willing a thing into being.
8. Niraḫ, angry god, (your) presence in the reeds is a serious matter (for) no one can find or see (you).
9. Enki-Niraḫ, (your) major presence in the reeds is a serious matter (for) no one can find or see (you).
10. Being attentive to that man, he has elevated him and granted him wisdom.
11. In the nation his given name has he made great.
12. They have caused there to be pasturage and irrigation for the black-headed, the living creatures as many as there are.

13–14. The *gudug*-priest administers divine oaths and so his bestowing the favorite things of the heart they grant for him.

15–16. The gods have brought into being the lion, the wild cat, and the dragon, his favorite things.

17. Praise, care, and merry-making!

18. May Enki-Niraḫ control whatever(?) snakes (there be).
19. Enki-Niraḫ grant … of Gungunum extensive wisdom!

NOTES

1. For the expression dumu-tab "twin sons," cf. Proverb Collection 2 no. 160 (Alster, *Proverbs* I, p. 75): é dumu tab dù a ḫé-me-en "May you be (a member) of a house built by twins." The third-singular verb -àm may reflect either maš-tab-ba being understood as singular or Enki-Niraḫ as one entity.

2. The poet has reversed the order of the names to emphasize that the two are twins, and thus equal. For the verb i denoting the birth of twins, cf. Proverb Collection 8 Sec. B no. 25 (Alster, *Proverbs* I, p. 170): ka$_5$ máš-bi mu-<šub> máš-tab-ba-ni mu-ni-in-i-i "The fox dropped her young. Her twins came out."

3. Presumably nir-ĝál refers to Niraḫ and mud to Enki. Perhaps the two different forms of the verb in the same verbal chain are intended to highlight that Niraḫ and Enki are the same (ša-an-), yet different (-du$_{11}$, -e).

4. maḫ dib can denote actual motion, "to pass along majestically," as in "Inana and Enki," line 227: sila-a maḫ ḫu-mu-un-dib "grandly pass along the street." However, it also may have the sense of "exceedingly great," as in "Ninurta's Exploits," line 707: in-nin me á-bi-ta è-a du$_{11}$-ge maḫ dib-ba "the lady who goes out with the divine powers, whose utterance is exceedingly great" (though here two verbs of motion are contrasted, è and dib).

5. This duplicates line 14 in Gungunum Hymn A: […] x niĝin$_2$-na-bi saĝ èn-tar-bi-me-en. For kur ki-sud-rá-šè and a similar line construction note Išme-Dagan H, line 12: kur ki-sud-rá-šè sipa-zi-bi za-e-men.

   For a waterway as zi-ĝál-kalam-ma, note Rīm-Sîn G, line 33: ^{id}nun ^{id}nun zi íd zi-ĝál kalam-ma "The Nun-canal, the reliable Nun-canal, the canal, the life(-giving force) of the nation."

6. The phrase en gal-zu níĝ-nam occurs elsewhere. Note Ninisina E, line 21: ^{d}Nin-isin$_2$-na en gal-zu níĝ-nam-ma "Ninisina, lord wise in all matters." The god An is called en-gal-zu in Rīm-Sîn C, line 7: an gal maḫ an ki-a en níĝ-nam gal-zu "Great An, majestic in heaven and earth, lord wise in all matters." Utu is also called en gal-zu in Hymn to Utu (B), line 24: en

gal-zu eš-bar dumu ^{d}En-líl-lá-ke$_4$ "Lord, wise one, decision-maker, child of Enlil."

7. The same phrase occurs in the *Temple Hymns*, line 284: Gú-ab-ba^{ki} šà-zu nîĝ ù-tu.

8. For lipiš "angry" said of gods, note "Inana's Descent," wherein it is said of Enlil and Nanna when responding to Ninšubur. Most certainly "angry" is appropriate for describing the snake aspect of the deity.

10. ĝeštug, as opposed to {ĝeš-túg}ĝeštug, perhaps should be understood as "ear," not "wisdom." Thus we have translated "attentive." Although "ear" can be written either ĝeštug or {ĝeš-túg}ĝeštug, "wisdom" seems to always be written with the frozen gloss, {ĝeš-túg}ĝeštug. This latter form may be the scribal way of honoring Wisdom, the very essence of their profession. They don't wish to "short change" wisdom by writing it the short way, PI, although, of course, the word for "wisdom" derives from "ear," listening (and thereby learning). This line seems to be an intentional paralleling between ĝeštug ĝar "to listen" and umuš ĝar "to grant wisdom," the former leading to the latter.

Cf. Šulgi B, line 177: lú-ulu$_3${lu} ní-te-a-ni-šè {ĝeš-túg}ĝeštug ḫé-ĝá-ĝá "People should consider for themselves."

12. Similar phrasing occurs in Samsuiluna E, line 18: saĝ-ĝi$_6$ zi-ĝál a-na lu-a ú-a-šè laḫ$_5$-laḫ$_5$-e.

13. For zi diĝir-ra as a divine oath, cf. CT 17 34: 35 (CAD N/2 290 *s.v. nīšu* A): zi-diĝir-gal-gal-e-ne-ke$_4$ ní ba-ra-nu-tuk-a *ša nīš ilī rabûti la ipallaḫu* "He who does not fear an oath by the great gods." We are unaware of the phrase zi du$_{11}$ in reference to oaths; the usual expression for taking an oath is zi pà. However, here, the gudug-priest, not lú, may be the subject of the verb du$_{11}$ and so the priest is not swearing an oath, but rather facilitating the man in taking the oath. Thus we have translated du$_{11}$ here as "administer."

14. Seemingly the subject of the verb ĝal is Enki and Niraḫ. If our translation of the line is accurate, then it declares that good things follow upon the taking of a divine oath.

15–16. For another attestation of these three creatures mentioned together note Gudea Cyl B iv, 20–21: ur-maḫ piriĝ ušumgal eden-na-ka ù dùb ĝar-ra-àm "the lions, wild cats, and dragons of the steppe were lying asleep." In our text these three creatures either parallel or comprise níĝ-sa$_6$-ga-a-ni "his favorite things." This may be understood in either of two ways. Perhaps this threesome, as witnessed in the Gudea Cylinder, was well-known imagery and so, perhaps, our scribe may have felt no need to expand upon the meaning of the imagery. Another possibility is that this passage refers to statues or decorations at Gungunum's palace, a synecdoche of his accomplishments and wealth.

Perhaps emend the text to: zà-mí <<mí>> du$_{11}$-ga.

18. a-na as an interrogative does not fit our context, although a-na in the expressions a-na ĝál and a-na me-a "whatever" (PSD A1 118–19) would be appropriate: "whatever snakes there be." If so, perhaps the scribe understood the ĝál in the verbal form at the end of the sentence as serving in a dual capacity, thus omitting it in a-na ĝál. a-na "in his waters" might also make sense.

For šu ĝál "to control," note, e.g., "Dumuzi and Ĝeštinana," line 70: ^{urudu}ḫa-zi-in šu ĝál, "to wield an ax," and Rīm-Sîn B, line 5: gi-kù-ga šu ĝál-le "who manipulates the holy reed-stylus."

19. The sign before the possessive form of the name Gungunum is very difficult to discern; its basic outline is rectangular. Our "best guess" is É, thus "the dynasty(?) of Gungunum," though this would be highly unusual.

YBC 7806 obverse

YBC 7806 obverse, lines 1 to 8

YBC 7806 obverse, lines 9 to 17

YBC 7806 reverse

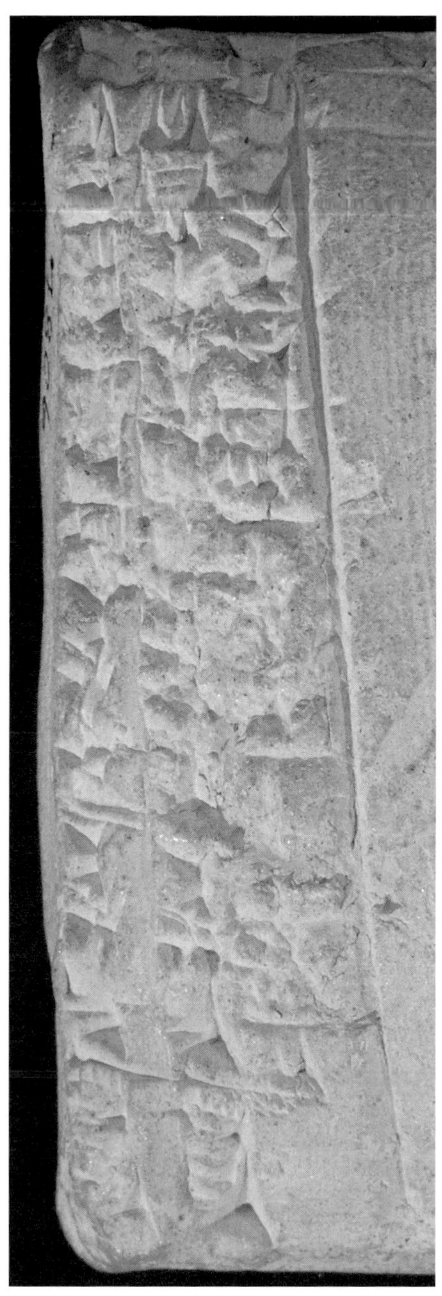

YBC 7806 reverse

That is part of the beauty of all literature. You discover that your longings are universal longings, that you're not lonely and isolated from anyone. You belong.

F. Scott Fitzgerald

3. A Harvest(?) Hymn to Nanna for King Sîn-iddinam

This hymn may have been composed in response to the harvest, either asking Nanna that the harvest go well or thanking him for the bounty. We offer this possibility based on two sections of the hymn. Lines 5–9 read:

> The harvest work(?), the extensive work of heaven and earth,
> has brought prosperity everywhere.
> Sacred harvest time, the important work of heaven and earth,
> at its glistening lustrations
> has Dilimbabbar, the royal son, joyously served.

Lines 41–42, at the close of the composition, read:

> .... bring forth ... gladly bring forth magnificently(?) the first produce (of) the field ... bring forth abundance, bring forth "Hurrah!"

An interesting aspect of this prayer to Nanna in so far as the creative process is concerned is its similarity to part of the later hymn to the moon-god for King Rīm-Sîn, known as Rīm-Sîn G. Lines 12–17 of our hymn correspond to lines 3–7 of Rīm-Sîn G.

The scribe divided this text into four sections, each separated by a line drawn across the tablet, but did not write any literary label naming the section type. The first three sections end with the refrain "Sîn-iddinam, my king!" although the closing line of the first section has additional text. Unfortunately, the fourth section is, but for a few signs, destroyed. The scribe of our text seems to have been extremely sloppy: signs are omitted (ll. 19, 21), lines are clearly corrupt (ll. 26–31), signs are not fully written (ll. 16–17, 22, 34), and words scrambled (l. 34).

The structure of the hymn is as follows.

SECTION ONE

Lines 1–4:	Standard royal introduction
Lines 5–11:	Nanna and Ningal preside over the harvest ritual
Lines 12-17:	Nanna and Ningal accept the king's gifts and prayers
Lines 18–27:	Nanna has established his house, from which he does good for the king, proclaiming his greatness and good fortune.

SECTION TWO

Although corrupt, these lines seem to be an exhortation that there always be plenty of food and drink, either for Nanna or for the king and or country.

SECTION THREE

The gods protect and bless the king

SECTION FOUR

(destroyed)

Text NBC 5452
130 × 65 × 25

Copy published in YOS 22, pls. XXXII–XXXIII, no. 23

1. ti-la lugal-mu p[à-da-^{d}En-líl-lá]
2. ki-áĝ-^{d}EN.[ZU]
3. ^{d}EN.ZU-i-dì-nam lug[al-m]u
4. pà-da-^{d}En-líl-lá ki-áĝ-^{d}EN.Z[U]
5. ⸢kíĝ$^{?}$⸣ buru$_{14}$ kíĝ-daĝal an-ki-a
6. nam-ḫe mi-ni-ĝar-ĝar
7. u$_{4}$-buru$_{14}$-kù kíĝ-dugud an-ki-a
8. šu-luḫ-dadag-ga-a-bé
9. ^{d}Dil-ím-babbar dumu-nun ḫúl-la-bi mi-ni-in-gub
10. ^{d}Ga-ša-an-gal-e nita$_{3}$-dam-ki-áĝ
11. siškur$_{2}$-re mi-ni-in-sikil
12. níĝ-dím-dím-kù ḫar-kù-zi-ge x x šu-sikil tag-ga-a-zu
13. šà-ga du$_{11}$-ga eme ĝar-ra-zu
14. šu-kù íl-la-a-zu

15. ^{d}Nanna lugal-an-ki-a
16. en ^{d}Lama$_{2}$-sa$_{6}$-ga-zu ḫu-mu-še$_{21}$$^{!}$(NÚ)-še$_{21}$$^{!}$(NÚ)
17. ^{d}Nin-gal nin-maḫ nin-ĝiškim-sa$_{6}$ zu ḫu-mu-še$_{21}$$^{!}$(NÚ)-še$_{21}$$^{!}$(NÚ)
18. ki me-lem$_{4}$ du$_{5}$-la-na ḫur-saĝ-gal in-ĝar
19. ki-nú šà-ḫúl-la <al> du$_{11}$-ga
20. dadag-ga babbar-ra me<-lem$_{4}$> dul-dul
21. šu da-ri-šè šu mi-ni-in-ĝar
22. šu-dadag(UD.<UD>) ma-ra-di-dam
23. saĝ íl ma-ra-ĝar-ĝar
24. si-ĝar-zu é-e šà-abzu ì-gi$_{4}$
25. nam-gal ma-ra-an-du$_{11}$
26. lugal-mu$^{!}$(nam) nam ma-an-ra-diri-ga
27. ^{d}EN.ZU-i-dì-nam lugal-mu$^{!}$(nam) nam ma-an-ra-[diri-ga]

---

28. ti-la lugal-mu a šu-zu kù-ge-eš ḫé-en-na-túm
29. ú zu-šè kù-ge-eš ḫé-en-na-(*erasure*$^{?}$)-túm
30. a šu-zu šen-šen-na ḫé-en-na-túm
31. ú zu-šè dadag-ga ḫé-en-na-túm
32. ^{d}EN.ZU-i-dì-nam lugal-mu

---

33. ti-la lugal-mu ^{d}Lama$_{2}$ ki-gal-lum ki-gal-la
34. ^{d}Lama$_{2}$ ká-bar-ra ⸢x⸣ en-nun nun-ke-en
35. igi-zu-uš i-lim-ta ḫu-mu-zal-le
36. ĝiškim-sa$_{6}$-ga-zu gaba-zu mu-ni-ri
37. ^{d}Ḫa-ia$_{3}$ gaba-ĝál ^{d}Nanna-ke$_{4}$
38. ^{d}Nisaba nin ir-du$_{10}$-ga
39. ^{d}Nanna á-daḫ á-daḫ-zu ḫé-a
40. ^{d}Nanna IGI.DU IGI.DU-zu ḫé-a
41. [ḫul]-ĝál inim búr si-sá-eš dab-dab-bé {lu}ulu$_{3}$
42. [x x m]ú$^{?}$-mú$^{?}$ šà-ḫúl nesaĝ gana$_{2}$ ĜÌR mú-mú-da
43. [x x (x) ḫ]é-ĝál mú-mú-da ì mú-mú-da
44. [x x x x]-⸢x⸣ silim-ma ḫu$^{!}$-mu-ra-ab-bé
45. [^{d}EN.ZU-i-dì-nam] lugal-mu

---

46. [...] ⸢x x⸣

47. [... m]ú
48. [...] ⸢x⸣
49. [...] mú
50. [...] x

TRANSLATION

1. (Long) live my king, the one summoned [by Enlil],
2. the beloved of Sîn,
3. Sîn-iddinam, my king,
4. the one summoned by Enlil, the beloved of Sîn.
5. The harvest work(?), the extensive work of heaven and earth,
6. has brought prosperity everywhere.
7. Sacred harvest time, the important work of heaven and earth,
8. at its glistening lustrations
9. has Dilimbabbar, the royal son, joyously served.
10. Gašangal, the beloved spouse
11. has purified the offerings there.
12. Your silver ornaments, golden rings, and ...,
13. your thoughts and utterances,
14. and your holy prayers
15. may Nanna, king of heaven and earth,
16. the lord, your friendly guardian always accept (and)
17. may Ningal, the great lady (who) knows favorable omens always accept!
18. In his place covered with awesome radiance has he set a great mountain,
19. desirous of a place of repose, the heart's delight,
20. glistening and shining, always enveloped in awesome radiance,
21. he operates eternally there.
22. Causing you to go about with (ritually) clean hands,
23. he has continually made you honored.
24. At the house, he has planted your bolt into the very midst of the abzu.
25. He has proclaimed greatness for you.
26. <My> king, he has made *whatever there is* exceeding for you!
27. Sîn-iddinam my king, he has made *whatever there is* exceeding for you!

---

28. (Long) live my king! May he bring him piously ... water.
29. May he bring him piously ... food.
30. May he bring him in purity ... water.
31. May he bring him in holiness ... food.
32. Sîn-iddinam, my king!

---

33. (Long) live my king! May the guardian of the platform, the great place,
34. the guardian of the outer door, ..., the watchman (of) the assembly(?),
35. remain before you there, apart from (your) awesome radiance.

36–38. Ḫaya, the guard of Nanna, and Nisaba, the lady of sweet fragrances, have caused you to receive there your favorable oracle.

39. May Nanna the helper be your helper!
40. May Nanna the guide be your guide!
41. Dispelling and routinely seizing evil, a south storm!
42. … bring forth, so that ... gladly bring forth magnificently(?) the first produce (of) the field …
43. … so that ... bring forth abundance, bring forth "Hurrah!"
44. may … utter a blessing for you,
45. Sîn-iddinam, my king!

(remainder almost entirely missing)

NOTES

1. There are two options for parsing the line: (1) ti-la lugal-mu pàd-da "Long live my king, the one summoned by ..." or (2) ti-la lugal mu pàd-da "Long live the king, he whose name has been called by ...." We prefer the first option, since the opening line of sections two and three begin lugal-mu "my king." Note the parallel Šulpae A, line 8 in which MU occurs twice in this context: lú-gal-mu mu-zu ḫe-pàd-de "My king, may he call your name." Our scribe is quite sloppy and has omitted signs elsewhere. We cannot dismiss the possibility that he has omitted a second MU sign in our line.

8–11. We understand the antecedent of -bi to be the harvest, that is, lines 8–11 refer to ritual ceremonies performed during the harvest.

10. Note that although the scribe uses the Emesal form Gašangal here, he uses the Emegir Ningal in line 17. Emesal occurs nowhere else in the text.

11–12. These lines seem to be a widely divergent variant of the later Rīm-Sîn G, line 2: šu-kù-zu siškur$_2$-kù sikil-e ma-ra-tag-ga-zu.

12. For níĝ-dím-dím, "creation," note "Lament of Sumer and Ur," line 24: ^{d}Nin-tu-re níĝ-dím-dím-ma ni-zag bí-in-tag-a-ba "Nintu has scattered the creatures she created." Note the syllabic orthography kù-zi-ge for kù-sig$_{17}$ "gold."

Note that Rīm-Sîn G, line 3 has ĝeš-tag-ga šu-tag-tag-ga-zu.

17. Rīm-Sîn G, line 3 has the verbal form as ḫé-me-še-še, which indicates that our careless scribe intended to write the ŠE$_{21}$ sign (ḪU+NÚ), but wrote only the NÚ part. The ETCSL cites eight instances of the verb še$_{21}$ *nabû* in the precative and none has a reduplicated root and all use ḫé- or ḫa-. Therefore, we should not automatically conclude that the intended meaning of še$_{21}$ in our text is "to name," particularly since mu "name" is absent.

The only other instance of which we are aware of a duplicated verbal form še-še, apart from Rīm-Sîn G, is "Ninurta and the Turtle," line 34: ur-saĝ ^{d}nin-urta è-dè nu-mu-un-še-še "The hero Ninurta did not agree(?) to go out," which, from context, might be connected to še-ga *magāru* "to agree." Note also AN : *Anum* VII 96–97 (Litke, *A Reconstruction*, p. 226) for the variant god names ^{d}A-ra-zu-še-ga "Who listens to (or accepts) prayer" and ^{d}A-ra-zu-še-še-gal. However, variant god names frequently indicate only similarity of sound and are not reliable for establishing meaning equivalences of their elements, in this case the equation of še-ga with še-še.

For Ningal involved with omens, again note Rīm-Sîn G, line 7: šà ^{d}Nanna ^{d}Nin-gal-bi ĝiškim-sa$_6$-sa$_6$-ga "favorable omens in the hearts of Nanna and Ningal."

18–21. These lines may refer to Nanna's temple, in effect his presence in the land.

18. Note the unusual variant du$_5$-la for dul-la, even though the scribe correctly writes dul in line 20. This may be a case of our scribe "showing off."

19–20. The careless scribe seems to have omitted a sign in the same position in lines 19 and 20. We base our restoration first on the fact that du$_{11}$-ga by itself here seems to add no meaning and second, and more significantly, note the somewhat parallel Dumuzi-Inana D1, line 19: ki-nú šà-ḫúl-la al ba-an-du$_{11}$ ki-nú al ba-an-du$_{11}$ "She desires the couch of heart's joy, she desires the couch."

21. The significance of the initial šu is unclear to us. A term šu ... šu—ĝar would seem to be superfluous.

22. Although dàg(=UD) by itself can equal *ellu*, *namru*, Sumerian texts have šu-dadag, not šu-dàg and so we have emended this text written by a sloppy scribe. šu-dadag can denote ritually clean hands. It is parallel to šu-sikil in Nanna E, line 54. In the hymn Nanna A, line 10, the moon-god is described as having šu-dadag. So too in Lipit-Ištar A, line 23 the implication is ritually clean hands. Therefore, the intent of our line may be that Nanna has blessed the king by putting him in a perpetual state of ritual cleanliness.

26–27. These two lines are assuredly corrupt. We do not expect diri to be said in conjunction with nam "fate." Rather we believe that the original line may have been lugal-mu níĝ-nam ma-ra-an-diri-ga, understanding níĝ-nam as *mimma*. Note the proverb UET 6/2 380 (Alster, *Proverbs*, I, p. 325): a-na-àm ba-ab-diri "As to what more" and Rīm-Sîn H, line 9: x-ga šu ša-mu-u$_{8}$-du$_{7}$ nam-zu ba-diri.

28–31. The scribe is quite sloppy throughout the text and something is clearly missing or wrong in this *kirugu*. Both the subject and the indirect object of the verb are in the third person. The verbal form ḫé-en-na-túm said of a "water," as perhaps in our text, occurs in Dumuzi-Inana T, line 5: a ḫé-en-na-túm a ḫé-en-na-túm numun zíz ĝi$_{6}$-ga "Let him bring her water, let him bring her water, and black emmer seeds." However, Sîn-iddinam is addressed throughout our composition in the second person, making it difficult to reconcile with our verbal form. The -zu in these lines would suggest the writer is addressing Sîn-iddinam in the second person as elsewhere.

The parallelism in this *kirugu* is evident. a "water" and ú "food" are frequently used in parallel in the literature (see ETCSL). The verb ḫé-en-na-túm occurs in each line. And the terms šen-šen-na, kù-ge-eš, and dadag-ga (all Akkadian *ellu*) are parallel. The parallelism between kù-ge and šen-šen occurs also in Išme-Dagan K, line 39: gi-gun$_{4}$-na-bi šen-šen-e-dè barag-bi kù-ge-dè "to purify their raised temples and to sanctify their daises." Finally, the remaining, puzzling elements šu-zu and zu-šè seem to be parallel, at least in position and in sound: /šz/ /zš/.

It seems unlikely that in line 28 šu-zu "your hand" (if that is what it means) is the subject of the verbal form, since the parallel line 29 has zu-šè instead with the same verbal form. Moreover, a translation "May your hand bring to him" hardly makes sense in our context.

For a šen "clear water," note "Lugalbanda and Anzu," line 389: ì-ne-éš íd šen-na íd a šen-na-ka.

Lastly, although the text includes some syllabic orthographies (kù-zi-ge, nun-ke-en), we believe it unlikely, particularly in light of the apparent parallelism, that ú-zu-šè here is syllabic for u_4-zu-šè "for all your days," as in Rīm-Sîn C, line 25: iti_6 níĝ-$giri_{17}$-zal šà-ḫúl-la u_4-zu-šè ḫu-mu-ra-ab-ĝar "May he establish moonlight, the happy and joyous thing, for you all your days."

33. Akkadian *kigallu* is a raised cultic platform, pedestal, or base of a statue. Sumerian ki-gal = *kigallu* is lexically attested. However, aside from our text, the only other attestation of ki-gal-lum is Šulgi C, line 46: maš-$dara_3$ ki-gal-lum-ma "cuneiform inscriptions on pedestals."

34. Our passage has some similarity to part of Rīm-Sîn F, line 37, which has en-nu-un ká-bar-ra, "watchman of the outer door," and note that $^{d}lama_2$, as in our text, occurs throughout that section of Rīm-Sîn F.

The surface of the tablet is partially destroyed after -bar-ra, but there is visible the top of a very small raised sign. The remaining part consists of two short horizontal wedges before at least three short vertical wedges, as in the NIR sign.

We suggest that the unusual writing en-nun-nun-ke-en is for en-nun unken, "watchman (of) the assembly." As we can see from the above quote from Rīm-Sîn F, line 37, en-nun should be "watchman, guard." Thus, we surmise that en-nun unken /ennununken/ became en-nun-nun-ke-en, also /ennununken/. One major drawback to our suggestion is that we then expect the genitive, unken-na. Most certainly, one would expect a place of assembly, whether divine or human, to have guards posted.

35. For -ta zal, cf. "Ninurta's Exploits," line 300: kur-ra u_4-ta im-ma-ra-zal "The day came to an end."

36–38. We don't expect the finite verbal form mu-ni-ri to precede the subject, presumably Ḫaya (with the ergative marker) and Nisaba in the next two lines, but this seems to be the case.

If Nisaba is related to the oracle in line 36, then ir du_{10}-ga may refer to sweet-smelling incense (see CAD E 280 *s.v. erešu* A mng. c) that might have been part of the oracular ritual.

42. ḫuš hardly seems appropriate here. Perhaps read ĝìr "to be magnificent" (CAD Š/2 37 *s.v. šarāḫu* A).

41. For inim búr "to dispel (evil)," see PSD B 193 *s.v.* bur_2 E mng. 3. For ḫul-ĝál dab_5-dab_5 note Martu A, line 19: ní-maḫ-a-ni ḫul-ĝál dab_5-dab_5-bé ulu_3{lu} "Acute fear of him seizes all the wicked … the south storm." Our line seems to have much in common with that passage. Our text seems to have {lu}ulu_3 instead of the expected ulu_3{lu}, and, if we have transliterated correctly, we can cite this as another example here of poor scribal practice.

44. The sign we have read ḫu- actually appears to be a RI sign.

The difference between literature and journalism is that journalism is unreadable and literature is not read.

Oscar Wilde

4. A Hymn to Utu for King Rīm-Sîn

The name of the king for whom the hymn was composed occurs in line 12 of the obverse:

[....-^{d}E]N.ZU sipa šà-ga ^{d}Utu

Owing to the many years of Rim-Sîn's reign and the fairly large number of hymns attributed to his reign, it seems quite likely that this too dates to Rīm-Sîn I, rather than to the reign of Warad-Sîn or even Bur-Sîn.

Line 11 is truly intriguing: DUMU.SAL I-a-ma-DIĜIR The Amorite name Yama'el "Yam is god" is elsewhere attested. Because the context unfortunately is broken, its significance here is unclear. Perhaps it is the name of a daughter of Rīm-Sîn, though a Yam name would be unexpected. But if so, perhaps she was in the service of the sun god, which could explain her presence in a hymn to Utu. So too, we might translate "the daughter of Yama'el (or Yama-ilum)," though we would hardly expect to find a personal name of someone not in the royal family in a royal hymn.

As best we can determine in lieu of all the breaks and missing lines, the structure of the work is as follows.

Lines 1–10:	Glorification of the sun god and description of the bounty he has brought the land.
Lines 11–12:	King Rīm-Sîn and his daughter are mentioned, though the context is broken.
Lines 13–18:	Broken
Lines 19–25:	Seems to refer to Utu and kingship.
Lines 26–37:	Missing
Lines 38–:	Our understanding of this section is quite tentative. The moon-god Suen assigns authority over kingship to his son, Utu, who, in turn, assumes responsibility for continually monitoring its exercise. Much of the remaining text refers to

bad acts and punishment. This section may be a general warning of Utu's punishment of any ruler who would abuse his position or who would contemplate hostile acts against Rīm-Sîn. Line 41 seems to begin the punishments, but lacks a smooth and logical transition from the previous line.

Forty-five years ago this tablet was identified as being in a very bad state of preservation, much of the surface flaking. To halt further deterioration a sealant was applied at that time. Although the flaking was arrested, the sealant poured into all the crevices and wedge indentations on the tablet. The result is that the tablet today is quite difficult to read. In many cases there remain only slight traces or a few wedges of the original sign and quite often blotches of sealant obscure the details that would enable clearer recognition of the sign. As a result, much of our transliteration is extremely tentative.

Text YBC 9869

133×91×34

obv.

1. [e]n-˹ḫuš˺ sa$_6$-ga kù-ga ˹an-ki-a-me-en˺ [gal]am$^?$ ˹ul-le˺-eš ˹kù-ga˺
2. ˹en-ḫuš˺ u$_4$-ḫuš a-si-ga šu-ta dé-dé ulutim$_2$ bàr-bàr-ra-ga
3. ˹u$_4$-ḫuš˺$^?$ di-di šilam-sa$_6^?$-ga [tù]r-[r]a u$_8$ amaš-bi ḫe-nun-na
4. ˹á-úr˺-sig$_7$-ga KA(×X$^?$)-x-maḫ (x x) ˹x˺-ta-˹a˺$^?$-da ˹nin-a˺-ni-ir túm-ma
5. ˹zà˺$^?$-ga-sig saĝ-ki-bi lum-lum mùš-bi zal-zal izi ĝiri$_3$-bar nu-tuk-a
6. ù zi-dè nu-nú ˹ká$^?$ šà$^?$-ge$^?$˺ mùš-bi u$_4$ ù-tu ù-ma mu-gub$^?$-bé
7. (x) x ˹$^{ĝeš?}$˺gigir-˹maḫ$^?$˺ galam kad$_4$-kad$_4$-da-ni-ta še-bi dub$^?$-dub$^?$-bé ĝá-nun-bé
8. [x x x x] dili-du èn-tar-sig$_7$-ga-zu téš nu-ĝál nu-mu-zu-zu
9. [x x x x] ˹x˺ nam-tag-dugud-da lú šu-ta nu-um-kar-re
10. [x x x x x x] ˹x˺-ma-ta níĝ-sa$_6$-ga-bi du-rí-šè bí-ĝál-la
11. [x x x x x x] ˹x˺ x (x) dumu-munus i-a-ma-DIĜIR
12. [x x x x ^{d}Ri-im-^{d}E]N.ZU sipa šà-ga ^{d}Utu
13. [x x x x x x]-ma
14. [x x x x x x] ˹ki/di$^?$˺ ˹ki˺-x-ka
15. [x x x x x x] ˹x˺ bí-in-ĝar-ra-a
16. [x x x x x x x x]-˹bi$^?$-šè$^?$˺ bí-in-sì-ga

17. [x x x x x x x x] maḫ$^{?}$ íb-ta-an-è-a
18. [x x x x x x x] diĝir-gal-gal-e-ne inim im-mi-in-gi$_4$
19. [x x x x x na]m-lugal-la-ka-ni
20. [x x x] en na-de$_5$ en-zi-uru$_{18}^{?}$-na-x
21. [x] ⸢gi$^{?}$⸣ [x] ⸢x⸣ x a-a ^{d}En-líl-lá-ka
22. [x x x gab]a-ĝál-la me$^{?}$-nam$^{?}$-nun-na-ni-a
23. [x x] ⸢x x⸣-na ki ĝál-la rig$_7$-ge-eš-⸢x⸣
24. [x x] ⸢x⸣ ki-ĝar-ra bara$_2$-maḫ nam-lugal-la
25. [x x x]-kù-kù-ga ní-bi bí-in-su$_8$-ga
26. [x x x] ⸢šà⸣$^{?}$-ḫúl-la u$_4$ mu-ni-ib-zal-zal-e-⸢ne⸣$^{?}$
27. [x x x] a-gàr-gal-gal-ta še gu-nu a ĝar-ĝar-ra
28. [x x x x] ⸢gi⸣$^{?}$ šu-peš giri$_{17}$-zal è[n]$^{?}$-šè i-ni-in-ĝál
29. [x x x šà-ini]m$^{?}$-ma-na du-rí-šè bí-in-du$_{11}$-ga
30. [x x x š]à$^{?}$ dub-ba šul ^{d}Utu-kam
31. [x x x x] ⸢x⸣-ni bí-in-ĝar-ra
32. [...] unu-gal
33. [...] x du$_{11}$-ga
34. [...] KA$^{?}$ NE$^{?}$
35. [...] ⸢x⸣ [x]
36. [...] ⸢x⸣ [x]

(remainder of obverse not preserved)

rev.

37. [...] ⸢x x x⸣ [...]
38. $^{[d]}$⸢EN⸣.ZU dumu-saĝ-⸢^{d}En-líl-lá-ke$_4$⸣ x-ra$^{?}$ lugal-kur-kur-ra-ke$_4$
39. ⸢bara$_2^{?}$⸣-ga-ni šu-na ù-mu-ni-in-[ĝar$^{?}$]
40. ⸢nam$^{?}$-lugal$^{?}$⸣ u$_4$-da⸣-ka-ni igi ḫu-mu-ni-íb-du$_8$-e
41. ⸢u$_4^{?}$⸣-na]m-ti-la-na ú zé-zé igi ḫé-bí-in-gi$_4$
42. [x x ḫé$^{?}$]-⸢ĝál⸣-e kalam-da mu-⸢da⸣-kar
43. [x] ⸢x⸣ sikil$^{?}$-le-da šu ḫé-en-dag-dag-ge
44. [x x] ⸢x⸣-ga-ni igištu(IGI.ŠÈ.DU) di-ku$_5$-maḫ an-ki
45. [x (x)] ki-ta an-ta al-du-e-re
46. [x (x)] ⸢ki$^{?}$-sukud$^{?}$-da$^{?}$⸣-ni-ta ù-mu-ni-in-šub-bé
47. [x] ⸢x⸣ ù$^{?}$ ⸢(x) x⸣ kù$^{?}$ ù-mu-ni-in-tìl
48. [x x] kar-re lú-bi-ta lú-kúr-ra ḫé-bí-íb-dab
49. [x x] ⸢x⸣ mir-du nu-kúš-ù ušum dili-du gaba-gi$_4$ nu-tuk-a

50. [x x] ⸢x⸣-ma?-ta ĝál na-an-da-da$_{13}$-da$_{13}$
51. [x x] ki?-a ba-da-dúb-dúb-bé ⸢mè?⸣ šen-na-aš bí-íb-te-ĝá
52. x x x x udug ḫul-ĝál saĝ nu-túm-mu
53. [x] ⸢x ḫe?⸣-nun-na-⸢ke$_4$⸣ [x] ⸢x⸣ [x] ⸢lugal?⸣-la ù-mu-ni-in-dab
54. [x x] ⸢x x ĝizzal⸣ ḫé-aka-ne
55. [x x x] ⸢x⸣ gaba ĝál ĜÌR.NITA$_2$ na de$_5$ kur ra ke$_4$
56. [na]m?-lugal ⸢kur? x x x⸣ ḫé-bí-íb-ur$_4$-re
57. [na]m?-lugal ⸢x x⸣ [x x] ḫé?-bí-íb-ak?-ak?-e
58. [na]m?-lugal ti?-la ⸢x⸣ [x] ⸢x x x⸣-ra-ni ur$_5$? nu-ug$_5$-ga
59. [… n]u?-me-a-bi
60. [… ĝi]ri$_3$ ḫé-bí-íb-gub-bé
61. […]-⸢x⸣ ní-zu igi íl-la
62. […] na-m]e saĝ nu-šúm-mu
63. […] x e-ne-du$_{11}$?
64. […] x zà? bí-in-keše$_2$
65. […]-íb-sa$_6$?
66. […]-⸢ni⸣?-íb-ur$_4$-⸢ur$_4$⸣
67. […bí]-íb-tur-re
68. […]-in-⸢x⸣
69. […]-⸢ur$_4$?-ur$_4$?⸣ (x)

TRANSLATION

1. Intense [lor]d, the beautiful and pure one of heaven and earth are you—[cle]ver(?), joyful, and pure.
2. Intense [lor]d, intense daylight(?) spreading over living creatures (like) clear water pouring from a hand.
3. Wherever the intense daylight(?) goes (there is) an abundance of fine cows in the cattle pen and ewes in their sheepfold.
4. (With) beautiful limbs, great … worthy of his lady;
5. whose chin(?) and forehead shine, whose countenance glows, an uncontrollable fire.
6. He who never sleeps during good daylight (hours) and whose countenance at the midst of the gate(?) (of heaven) produces light stands in triumph.

7. From his skillfully fashioned great(?) chariot(?) piling up the barley at its storehouse.
8. The solitary …, he who inquires after your goodness will never know what it is to have no dignity.
9. … a serious crime, the man does not escape.
10. At … there will always be good things.
11. … daughter Yama'el.
12. … [Rīm]-Sîn, the favorite shepherd of Utu,
13. …
14. …
15. … set.
16. … placed.
17. … from … gone out,
18. … the great gods replied.
19. … his ... of kingship.
20. … the lord (who) gives advice, true towering(?) lord.
21. … of Father Enlil.
22. … forceful ... the *me* of his princeship(?).
23. … … presenting …
24. … erecting ..., the great dais of kingship.
25. … pure … itself stand.
26. … spend the time joyously.
27. … on the expansive fields watering the barley and flax.
28. How long shall there be … the largesse and jubilation?
29. … by the intent of his word he has decreed it forever.
30. It is … on a tablet of manly Utu.
31. … placed.
32. … great dining hall(?)
33. … spoken.
34. …
35. …
36. …
37. …
38. After Sîn, the firstborn of Enlil, the … of the king of all the lands,

39. has put his throne(?) under his control,
40. daily may he monitor kingship(?)!
41. May he transform the [days?] of his life into hacked plants!
42. [...] take away [abun]dance from the nation.
43. May ... be cut off (or: roam about)!
44. ... his ... the foremost one, the great judge of heaven and earth
45. After ... goes below and above,
46. after ... has fallen from his heights(?),
47. after ... has ended(?),
48. ... escape, from that man may the enemy seize it!
49. ... a *mirdu*-snake that does not tire, a solitary dragon that is unopposed,
50. ... does not open.
51. ... ground ... shakes, ... approaches battle.
52. ... the merciless(?) evil demon.
53. After ... of abundance(?) ... royal(?) ... seized,
54. may they pay attention ...!
55. May the forceful one, the commander, the advice-giver of the land
56. gather ... king[ship(?)] ...!
57. May he ... king[ship(?)] ...!
58. Should the kingship end(?), ... his ... not despair(?).
59. ... there not(?) be ...
60. May [...] step there!
61. ... see for yourself.
62. ... no] one can oppose.
63. ...
64. ... fastened at the side.
65. ... be good.
66. ... gather ...
67. ... limited.
68. ...
69. ... gather(?) ...

NOTES

1–3. The term en ḫuš occurs in an incipit in an Ur III catalogue at Yale: ur-saĝ en ḫuš gal. It occurs also as an epithet of the other great astral body, the moon (see herein 5:36). One cannot dismiss the possibility of reading uru$_{16}$ "mighty (one)," instead of en "lord." Note the three consecutive entries in OB Izi (PBS 12, 4, obv. iii 7'–9'): 7': u$_{18}$-ru 8': uru$_{16}$(EN) 9': ḫuš.

In the Old Babylonian period, the signs ḫuš and ĝìr (*gašru* "strong," *šarāḫu* "to be resplendent") are very difficult to distinguish and the poor condition of our text makes the task even more difficult. Thus we cannot totally discount a reading ĝìr at least in some places in these lines.

The term ḫuš modifies en and u$_4$ in our three lines and can have a meaning "red." In the context of the sun's appearance, consider *agû ruššû ša šamê* "red tiara of the sky" said of Utu (CAD R 429a). At times, the sun can appear to be red, particularly at sunrise and sunset, for at those two times of the day the sun is farthest away and so the sun's rays must travel a longer distance to reach us, creating the red-shift effect, the same effect that is used to determine the distance of stars from Earth. Thus translating here en-ḫuš, "the red lord," is conceivable, but since, as noted above, the moon is also called en-ḫuš, a translation here "red" is very unlikely.

The term u$_4$-ḫuš, as in lines 2 and 3, usually is translated "furious storm" and occurs, among other instances, as epithets of Inana ("The Death of Ur-Namma," line 204: u$_4$-ḫuš dumu-gal ^{d}Suen-na) and Ninurta (e.g., Šulgi T, line 19: ^{d}Nin-urta u$_4$-ḫuš izi er$_9$-ra nam-[...]), two deities whose personas could be described as "stormy." However, that does not seem to be the case with Utu in literature, although one can argue that u$_4$-ḫuš is just a standard epithet that can be applied to any deity, regardless of the god's true nature. Still, in the case of Utu, the sun, for two reasons one should consider u$_4$ to mean "daylight" in our context. First, the verb bara$_3$, as in line 2, is elsewhere said of light, "to spread light," but not said of a storm. Second, our lines 2 and 3 are very positive in describing the effect of the sun. Understanding u$_4$ here as "storm" does not fit that context.

Moreover, if u$_4$ here indeed is "daylight," then ḫuš in u$_4$ ḫuš should not mean "red," since, although the sun may appear to be red at times, the daylight does not.

Therefore, we have understood ḫuš here as *ezzu*. Because of Utu's nature, we have translated "intense," that is, having intense feelings in a positive manner, a nuance not conveyed by the word "furious." However, note that in 5:36 the epithet en-ḫuš of the moon seems to come closer to "furious lord," since the moon is described as brandishing a weapon in that passage.

2. The expression a-si-ga dé, "to pour clear waters," occurs also in "The Incantation to Utu," line 167: a-si-ga na-an-dé-a with a syllabic-text version a-si-ga na-di (PSD A/1 164).

3. Although di-di is most likely "to go," a remote possibility is that di-di may be for di_5-di_5 *nabāṭu* "shine."

4. The phrase "beautiful limbs" is used in two texts to describe Gilgameš. Note "Gilgameš and the Bull of Heaven," line 3: á-úr-sag_9-sag_9 šul mè-ka en-du-ni ga-an-du_{11} "I will sing a song of beautiful limbs, of a young man of war," and "The Death of Gilgameš," line 3: á-úr-sa_6-sa_6 (...) ba-nú ḫur nu-mu-e-da-an-zi-zi "He of beautiful limbs lay down, never to rise again."

5. For zag-ga "chin," see CAD K 172 *s.v. kanzūzu*. "Chin" here complements "forehead," i.e., his head from bottom to top. zag-ga, of course, just means "side," and specifies the chin, at least in the lexical texts. Our term zag-ga sig "the lower side" seems a more accurate term for specifying the location of the chin.

   For lum "to shine," see CAD N/1 210 *s.v. namāru*. Cf. to our line Nanna C, line 4: nun x-AŠ saĝ-ki-bi lum-lum mùš-bi x [...] and "Gilgameš and Aga," line 111: saĝ lum-lum nun an-né ki-áĝ "he with a shining forehead/head, beloved by An." Both saĝ-ki and saĝ are lexically equated to *pûtu* "forehead," "front of the head."

   For the expression $\hat{g}iri_3$-bar nu-tuku *ša kišdam la išû* "limitless," see CAD K 450 *s.v. kišdu*.

6. For ù zi "good daylight," cf. Nanna N, line 13: e i lú-gal-mu ù zi ši-mu-nu, which the ETCSL translates: "Oh it has come forth for my king like the good sunlight."

   For the concept of Utu shining forth from the midst of a gate (ká šà-ge), note *libbi bābi in amēlūti Šamaš ina libbi bābi aṣêšu īmuru* "mankind saw Šamaš at the gate where he comes forth" (CAD B 22 *s.v. bābu* A).

7. The concept of the chariot of the sun is, of course, common across cultures. For the Mesopotamian tradition, see CAD N/1 357 *s.v. narkabtu* mng. 1d. If read correctly, our line describes the bounty that Utu provides to the nation.

9. For the construction nam-tag dugud šu-ta, cf. Nungal Hymn, line 80: nam-tag dugud šu-ta im-sig-ge-en "I temper severe punishments."

11. For occurrences of the West Semitic personal name Yama'el, "Yam Is God," see Streck, *Onomastikon*, p. 272.

14. The sign before -ka looks like BARAG, but, if so, we would expect barag-ga.

16. For a construction perhaps similar to ours, cf. Ur-Ninurta B, line 7: me an-ki saĝ keše$_2$-bi-šè ma-ra-an-sì "He has laid upon you (Enki) the guarding of the *mes* of heaven and earth." Perhaps this line is describing something that Utu has bestowed upon Rīm-Sîn.

20. Although en-zi here is probably "true lord," it could also be *ašaridu*, frequently said of animals (see ePSD). For en-uru$_{18}$-na, note, e.g., "Enlil and Ninlil," line 146: en-uru$_{18}$-na za-e-me-en.

22. The wording gaba-ĝál me-nam-nun-na occurs in two other texts: "The Instructions of Šuruppak," line 204: nir-ĝál-e níĝ-tuku gaba-ĝál me nam-nun-na "To have authority, to have possessions and to be forceful is a princely *me*"; and Išme-Dagan I, line 34: gaba-ĝál-zu me-maḫ nam-nun-na-kam "You forcefulness is the great *me* of princeship."

27. For somewhat similar passages with a-gàr-gal, note "Summer and Winter," line 34: a-gàr-gal-gal-ta a nam-ta-an-ĝar "He watered the great fields"; and Ur-Namma D, line 36: a-gàr-gal-bi še gu-nu mú-mú "its great fields growing barley and flax."

32. A meaning "tomb" for unu-gal here seems unlikely.

39–40. These two lines may be similar to "Enmerkar and the Lord of Aratta," line 399: x x šu-na um-ma-ni-in-ĝar igi um-ši-bar-bar "After he has it in hand and contemplates it."

40. For u$_4$-da-ka-ni "daily," cf. Inana C, line 211: nitaḫ munus-bi gu-dili-a mi-ri-è-dè níĝ u$_4$-da-ka-ni igi-zu-šè bí-íb-ta-lá" "Men and women go out before you as a single thread and dangle before you daily."

Cf. Proverb Collection 3.31, 6 (Alster, *Proverbs*, I, p. 86): nam-lugal-kala-ga igi nu-mu-du$_8$ "He never saw mighty kingship."

41. This line begins a series of curses or punishments, though the segue from the previous line seems weak, if at all existent. Presumably the following action is a result of Utu's vigilance over the abuse of kingship.

The first sign of the line is hardly visible, but it is quite narrow and the UD sign could fit the space and the slight traces. It would also create a word play between u$_4$ and ú and poignant imagery, that the days of his life be cut short like cut plants. In Ur III economic texts the task ú zé "plant cutting" is often assigned to workers.

igi—gi_4 means "to change the appearance." Cf. "Enlil and Namzitara," line 12: ^{d}En-líl-le igi-ni mu-ni-in-gi_4 "Enlil, changed his appearance" and The Nippur Lament, line 83: é ... ta-aš igi bí-in-gi_4 "Why did he change the appearance of the temple ...." Note the Akkadian idiom *panâ târu* (CAD T 274 *s.v. târu*), meaning unclear.

42. Cf. to our line, Ur Lament, line 173: u_4-ḫé-ĝál-la kalam-da ba-da-an-kar "the time of abundance has been taken from the nation."

43. šu—dag can be either "roam about" or "cut off, abandoned" (see ePSD). In light of the form -da kar in the previous line, note "Gilgameš, Enki, and the Netherworld," line 11: ibila ba-da-kar gidim-ma-ni šu al-dag-dag-ge." Actually, either translation of šu—dag is possible (ETCSL translates "roam about").

49. For mir-du nu-kúš-ù cf. "Ninurta's Exploits," line 3: a-ma-ru mir-du nu-kúš-ù ki-bal ĝá-ĝá "A flood, a *mirdu*-snake that never tires set against the enemy land." The reading mir-du is based upon the variant mir-tu (Heimpel, *Tierbilder*, p. 511, no. 98.5). For ušum dili-du cf. Šulgi E, line 216: ušum dili-du-gin_7 ní mu-da-ri "Like a solitary dragon that engenders fear."

51. Cf. a proverb from Ur, line 4: mè šen im-ma-te (Alster, *Proverbs*, I, p. 322).

52. CAD M/1 45a *s.v. magirtu*, states "the meaning of sag.túm as insult, insolence, is established" noting Emesal Voc. III 11 saĝ ir-ir = saĝ túm-túm = *qullulu marû*. However, it should be noted that in the Emesal Voc. the verb DU is replicated, unlike in our text. Moreover, DU has a reading ir_{10}, which may account for the Emesal equivalence. Also note Šulgi B, line 229: $šer_7$-da saĝ ì-túm-túm-ĝá, which indicates a positive action against crime. Neither of these references to saĝ túm seems germane to saĝ túm in our passage. Rather, perhaps saĝ nu-túm-mu here mirrors igi nu-túm-mu (*la bābil panī*) "merciless" in our composition 6:7.

55. We are unaware of any other occurrence of the epithet na-de_5 kur-ra. However, Nuska is called na-de_5 kalam-ma (Nuska A, line 5).

60. It is unclear whether $ĝiri_3$ is to be understood here as "foot," thus $ĝiri_3$—gub "to step," or as "path." Cf. "Letter from Inanaka to Nintinuga," line 21: ki-in-du ki nam-ti-la-ka $ĝiri_3$-mu ḫé-bí-íb-gub-bé(-en).

64. For zag $keše_2$, note "A Harvest(?) Hymn to Nanna for King Sîn-iddinam" (herein), line 14: nam-nir-ra zag $keše_2$ "clasping authority at his side."

YBC 9869 obverse

YBC 9869 obverse lines 1 to 17

YBC 9869 obverse lines 18 to 32

YBC 9869 reverse

YBC 9869 reverse lines 37 to 53

YBC 9869 reverse lines 54 to 69

5. The Fifteen Phases of the Moon

This hymn to the moon-god Suen is unique in that it ascribes particular manifestations of the moon to each daily phase for the first half of the month.

The beginning of the text is badly broken, but seems to be praise of Suen. At some point Suen is exhorted to reveal his names, presumably the names for his phase each day of the month. The reverse begins with a reference to the three major phases of the moon: the new moon, the moon on day 7 (half moon), and the moon on day 15 (the full moon). The following two lines may perhaps describe the new moon. Thereafter, each day up through the 15th of the month is specified and a different power or manifestation of the moon's "crown" (Sum. men). The longest passage, as one might expect, is reserved for the 15th, the full moon. Thereafter, the poet describes the moon's effect upon the cities and the reaction of other deities to his power.

Many gods are portrayed as wearing crowns, these crowns signifying authority and power. However, in the case of the moon, the term may involve more than just religious iconography. The term may also allude to the physical appearance of the moon. CAD T 112a mng. 2, in reference to the moon, translates men *agû* as "earthshine" (see note to line 26 below). Earthshine is the glow on that part of the moon that is not fully lit, i.e., the part that is mostly dark. Another possible interpretation of aga is the moon's corona, which is caused by light being diffracted from atmospheric droplets of water, producing a halo-effect around the moon. It is also conceivable that the crown refers to the actual moon itself, viewed as the god's adornment. However, our text plainly states in line 26': men igi-du$_8$-a-zu "the crown (is) your appearance," and so we suggest that the Sumerian term men in our text refers to the physical moon itself, rather than to the corona or some abstract concept.

The obverse is badly broken. The major portion of the reverse is preserved, though no line completely. Moreover, there is great abrasion to the surface, preserving only slight traces of many signs.

YBC 4650
107×66×29

obv.
(beginning destroyed but for sporadic traces)

1'. [...]
2'. [...] x [...]
3'. [...] x x x [...]
4'. [... na]m$^{?}$-⸢bi-šè⸣ mùš$^{?}$ m[á$^{?}$ ...]
5'. [...] ⸢x⸣ ku$_4$-ku$_4$ mu-un-šub ⸢x⸣ [...]
6'. [...]-⸢šà$^{?}$-ga⸣-ke$_4$ si-il-⸢lá⸣ m[u$^{?}$ ...]
7'. [...ni]n-kur-kur-ra-ke$_4$ kù ^{d}Nin-gal ⸢x⸣ [(x)]
8'. [...]-a-ni u$_4$-4-kam-ma u$_4$-múš$^{?}$-a-k[am-ma]
9'. [... igi$^{?}$-bi$^{?}$-šè$^{?}$ ḫi$^{?}$]-⸢li$^{?}$⸣ du$_8$-du$_8$ a-ga-bi-šè ul gùr-ru
10'. [...] asil$_3$-lá ba-te
11'. [...] ⸢x x x⸣ mu-un-sikil du$_{11}$-ga šà$^{?}$ bí-íb-dab$_5$
12'. [...] ⸢x x x x⸣-šè$^{?}$ ⸢bara$_2$$^{?}$⸣ zà-dib-ba mu-na-GUB
13'. [...] ⸢dúr$^{?}$ ba⸣-an-ĝar
14'. [...] ⸢x⸣ [... me-t]éš ḫu-mu-i-i
15'. [... du$_{11}$]-ga-zi-da-me-en
16'. [...]-bi za-e [x x x (x)] za-e-gin$_7$ dalla mu-[...]
17'. [...] ⸢x⸣-e nu-di-di ⸢x x⸣ [x x x] ⸢DU$^{?}$⸣-a-zu [x x] ⸢x⸣
18'. [...] u$_4$-sakar ^{d}EN.ZU-na-šè mu-un-ši-ḫúl ⸢x⸣ [x (x)]
19'. [(x) dumu-n]un-na a-a-zu ^{d}En-lil-lá mu-zu du$_{11}$-[ga-ab]
20'. [x x] x kù$^{?}$-ga$^{?}$ x x še-er-zi an-na kù [... mu-zu du$_{11}$-ga-ab]

bot.
21'. [ĝeš-n]u$_{11}$-gal mul-sa$_7$-a zalag-ge mu-zu du$_{11}$-ga-[ab]
22'. [x x dumu$^{?}$-nu]n$^{?}$-na$^{?}$ ama-zu ^{d}Nin-líl-e mu-zu du$_{11}$-ga-[ab]
23'. [x] ⸢x sa$_6$$^{?}$⸣-é-kur$^{?}$-ra ^{d}NIN-maḫ-e mu-zu d[u$_{11}$-ga-ab]
24'. [x]-⸢gal$^{?}$ $^{d?}$⸣EN$^{?}$.ZU$^{?}$ dalla-an-na ù-ma-ni sá-sá diĝir-re-e-[ne-ke$_4$ ...]
25'. [x x] ⸢^{d}EN$^{?}$.ZU$^{?}$ x⸣-an-kù-ga ⸢x x x x x⸣ [...]

rev.
26'. ĝeš-nu$_{11}$-gal-an-na men igi-du$_8$-a-zu ⸢u$_4$-sakar u$_4$-7 u$_4$-15-kam-ma⸣
27'. ⸢mul$^{?}$⸣-gal-gin$_7$$^{?}$ an-na níĝ-su-ub a-a [... men]-zu nam-en-na [x]

28'. en ĝeš-nu$_{11}$-gal-an-na men igi-d[u$_8$-a-zu …]-a ḫu-mu-un-⸢x⸣-[(x)]
29'. en an ki ušum-dalla […] men-zu u$_4$-2-kam-ma
30'. en me-lem$_4$ an-kù-ga [šú-a …] men-zu u$_4$-3-kam-ma
31'. en mul-sa$_7$-a z[alag-g]e (…) men-zu u$_4$-4-kam-ma
32'. en eri-bàd$^?$ [di]m$^?$-gal-an-ki-a men-zu [ ] en (x) u$_4$-5-kam-ma
33'. en er[i$^?$] ⸢imin$^?$ bi$^?$⸣ [m]ú a šu gal bi du$_7$ ú ⸢x⸣ [x x x] ga men-zu u$_4$-6-kam-ma
34'. ⸢en x-bi⸣ utaḫ$^?$-ḫé$^?$ ḫi-li gú è men-zu u$_4$-7-kam-ma
35'. en me-kù-ga šu-luḫ-zalag$_2$-ga <me>-sikil-la men-zu u$_4$-8-kam-ma
36'. en-ḫuš diĝir-re-e-ne x(-x) ak-e men-zu u$_4$-9-kam-ma
37'. en ní-gal-an-na ní me-lem$_4$ mú-mú men-zu u$_4$-10-kam-ma
38'. [en š]e-er-zi diĝir-re-e-ne-er pa è men-zu u$_4$-11-kam-ma
39'. ⸢en$^?$⸣ ĝeš-nu$_{11}$-dadag ĝišgal-bi an-na gub-ba men-zu u$_4$-12-kam-ma
40'. en an-na u$_6$-di an ^{d}En-líl gub-ba [me]n-zu u$_4$-13-kam-ma
41'. en ĝeš-búr-šè ĝe[š-eški]ri$_2$$^?$-šè me-ninnu du$_{11}$-ga men-zu u$_4$-14-kam-ma
42'. ^{d}EN.⸢ZU⸣-e men-zu u[du]g-[m]aḫ$^?$-an-ki-a ĝiri$_3$-zu-šè lugal gurum-ma men-zu u$_4$-15-kam-ma ḫé$^?$-e en-nu-un u$_4$ […-zal]
43'. ⸢x⸣-bi mùš me-lem$_4$-zu ⸢šu$^?$ du$_{11}$⸣-ga [ḫu]-luḫ-ḫa kur ĜAR-⸢x⸣ […]
44'. [ku]r$^?$-ra$^?$ ér-bi im gana bí-ib-si ĝi$_6$-a IM gal-bi […]
45'. diĝir-gal-⸢gal-e-ne men⸣-zu ḫé-eb-ri ⸢u$_4$$^?$-da$^?$⸣ a-a-z[u …]
46'. [(x) x me]n-zu an-daĝal-la ḫé-ni-ib-zal[ag …]
47'. ⸢ku$_4$-ku$_4$⸣-da-zu-šè ^{d}Lama$_2$ an-šà-ga ⸢x⸣ […]
48'. [ki-á]ĝ ^{d}En-líl-lá ka-tar si-il-l[a …]
49'. [diĝir-ga]l-gal-an-ki-ke$_4$-ne silim-ma z[i$^?$-dè-eš …-e]
50'. x x x a men-zu 5-⸢kam$^?$-ma$^?$ x⸣ [
51'. [ ] ⸢x⸣ UD ⸢x⸣ […]
52'. […] ⸢x⸣ […]
53'. […] ⸢x⸣ […]
54'. […] ⸢x⸣ […]
55'. […] ⸢x⸣ […]

(remainder not preserved)

TRANSLATION

(beginning not preserved)

4'. … to that end … surface(?) … bo[at …]
5'. … entering … has left ...
6'. … inspection(?) …
7'. … lady of the all lands, holy Ningal, …
8'. … his …, it is the fourth day; [it i]s] the day of (your) countenance(?).
9'. … [at its front(?)] filled with [ecsta]sy(?), at its rear covered in attractiveness.
10'. … approaches with joy.
11'. … made pure, (whose) utterance is taken to heart(?).
12'. … at ... the surpassing dais(?) stands ready to serve him.
13'. … has taken (his) place(?).
14'. May … utter praise!
15'. … you are the one of the true ut[terance].
16'. … you are …, like you ... shining.
17'. So that … do not go, … your ...
18'. … rejoices at (…of) the new moon, Suen.
19'. … prin[cely son] of your father Enlil, tell your name!
20'. … light of heaven, holy [... tell your name]!
21'. Great [lum]inary lighting up the darkness, tell your name!
22'. [Prin]cely(?) [son(?)], to your mother Ninlil tell your name!
23'. To the lovely(?) ... of the Ekur, Ninmaḫ, tell your name!
24'. Great(?) ..., Sîn(?), the shining one of heaven, the one of the gods who achieves his victories, ...
25'. Sîn(?), ... of holy heaven ...
26'. Great luminary of heaven, the crown (is) your appearance at the new moon, on day 7, and on day 15.
27'. Like(?) a great star(?) polishing the heavens […] your crown is lordship.
28'. Lord, great luminary of heaven, may the crown, your appearance, ….
29'. Lord ... heaven and earth ... glowing viper, ... is your crown on the second day.

30'. Lord whose awesome splendor [envelops?] the holy heavens, ... is your crown on the third day.

31'. Lord who lights up the darkness, … is your crown on the fourth day.

32'. Lord (of) the walled(?) city, the great axis of heaven and earth, is your crown on the fifth day.

33'. Lord who lights up all the cities(?), perfectly exercising authority, …, is your crown on the sixth day.

34'. Lord ... who clads the heavens(?) in allure is your crown on the seventh day.

35'. Lord of the holy *me*s, the glistening lustrations, the pure <*me*s> is your crown on the eighth day.

36'. Furious lord who ... the gods is your crown on the ninth day.

37'. Lord, awesome luminosity of heaven clad in dread and awesome splendor is your crown on the tenth day.

38'. Lord, light made manifest for the gods is your crown on the eleventh day.

39'. Lord, sparkling luminosity following its (true) path in the sky is your crown on the twelfth day.

40'. Lord, in heaven the marvel serving(?) An and Enlil is your crown on the thirteenth day.

41'. Lord who with (the authority of) the crook and nose-rope(?) controls the fifty *me*s is your crown on the fourteenth day.

42'. Oh Suen, your crown is the great(?) weapon of heaven and earth (causing) kings to bow at your feet. Indeed, it is your crown of the fifteenth day. You [spend] the day keeping watch.

43'. Your awesome appearance touches(?) its ... quaking ... the land …

44'. Whose tears fill the clouds(?) with rain(?) in the mountains(?), whose ... in the night.

45'. Indeed, your crown guides the great gods; during the day(?) your father, …

46'. Indeed, your [crow]n lig[hts up] the broad sky, …

47'. When you enter, the guardian of the interior of heaven …

48'. Beloved of Enlil, praised …

49'. The great gods of heaven and earth justly bless …

50'. ... your crown ... fifth ...
(remainder not preserved)

NOTES

4'. For nam-bi-šè "for that reason," cf. Šulgi G, line 15: nam-bi-šè é-kur-ra sig_7 mi-ni-ĝar ^{d}Dil-ím-babbar-re "To that end, Dilimbabbar appeared shining in the Ekur."

6'. Perhaps si-il-lá *piqittu* "inspection."

7'. We are unaware of any reference to Ningal with the epithet "Lady of all the lands." This title is given to Inana (e.g., Inana B, line 62); Nanaya (Išbi-Erra C, line 3); Nanše (Gudea Cyl A iv, 13); Ninisina (Iddin-Dagan A, line 21); and Ninlil ("Enlil in the Ekur," line 165). Thus, this seems to be a standard epithet given to any important goddess, rather than defining her unique position within the pantheon.

8'. Fort múš "countenance" see CAD Z 120 *s.v. zīmu* 2' for *zīmu* referring to the appearance of the moon and other heavenly bodies.

9'. Both me-lem_4 du_8-du_8 and ḫi-li du_8-du_8 are attested. There are two references to me-lem_4 du_8-du_8 and twelve references to ḫi-li du_8-du_8 cited by the ETCSL. Moreover, ḫi-li better parallels ul. Lastly, the ever-so faint traces slightly favor the LI sign rather than the LEM_4 sign. Thus we believe ḫi-li to be the more likely restoration.

11'. Cf. to our line, Šulgi B, line 158: ĝeš šu-kár-ke_4 šà bí-ib-dab_5.

16'. We expect è after dalla mu-.

19'–23'. For the expression mu-zu du_{11}-ga-ab, cf. Proverb Collection 5 (Alster, *Proverbs*, I, p. 128) no. 55, line 3: tukum bi šu mu ri bar re mu zu du_{11}-ga-ab "If I let you go, tell me your name."

19'. For the moon with the epithet dumu-nun-na, see Sjöberg, *Mondgott*, p. 142.

20'. For the moon indirectly called še-er-zi-an-na, cf. Gudea Cyl A xxvii, 10: še-er-zi-an-na-ka ì-ti-gin_7 è-a "coming out like the moonlight in the radiance of heaven."

21'. For mul-sa_7-a *ikletu* "darkness," see CAD I/J 60. Perhaps the reason this term is lexically equated to "darkness" is that when one can best see the stars in all their glory, it needs to be very dark outside.

23'. Although the reading ^{d}Nin-maḫ is widely accepted, see A. Cavigneaux and M. Krebernik, *RlA* 9, p. 462 for a syllabic reading indicating ^{d}Ereš-maḫ. We are unaware of Ninmaḫ's association with the Ekur. However, Ninmaḫ was identified with Ninḫursag, who did have a cult in Nippur (and who may, in turn, have been identified with Ninlil, the true mother of the Ekur) and so this may have been the source of Ninmaḫ's epithet in our passage.

24'. For ù-ma sá-sá, "to achieve victory," cf. Inana C, line 62: ^{d}Inana bàd ^{na_4}gul-gul [...] ù-ma sá-sá; "Hymn to Ninĝešzida," line 32: ur-saĝ ù-ma sá-sá. See CAD K 271 *s.v. kašādu* for DI.DI glossed sa-sa in several lexical texts. However, Antagal G 178 has the gloss sa-du for DI.DI, presumably reflecting sá-du$_{11}$, also equated to *kašādu*.

26'. The phrase men igi-du$_8$-a-zu is reflected in Akkadian*: tāmarti Sîn u agêšu* in the "Diviner's Manual" (CAD T 112a mng. 2); cf. also *šumma Sîn ina tāmartišu agâ apir* (ibid.).

27'. All five other literary references to níĝ-su-ub occur with the verb ak, and refer to polished metal (see ETCSL). Since the moon is addressed in the second person, we do not expect a-a-ni, "his father." Just perhaps a-a is for ak-a, thus níĝ-su-ub ak-a, as in the hymns Baba A, line 38 and Dumuzi-Inana T, line 16. For two other attestations of a for ak, note Gudea Cyl A xxvi 19: mu-bi ... pa è ba-ni-a "made their names appear"; Proverb from Susa: di inim ga-ra-du$_{11}$ {ĝeš.túg}ĝeštug ĝizzal ḫe-em-ši-a "Let me tell you about a legal matter and you should pay attention."

29'. The moon is referred to as ušum in several other texts. ušum is a viper *bašmu* or a mythological snake, but could also simply denote "foremost" *ašaredu* in all these references. Note Nanna L, line 18: ^{d}Nanna ušum an-ki and Ibbi-Sîn S, line 2: ^{d}Suen ušum saĝ-kal. We prefer a translation "viper" here, because on the second day the moon appears as a sliver, a long line that could resemble a curved snake.

30'. For this imagery of the moon in our line, note "Letter from X to Nanna," line 11: me-lem$_4$-zu an-kù-ga šú-a.

31'. See the note to line 21'.

32'. For eri-bàd, "walled city," cf., e.g., Šu-ilišu A 4: ^{d}Nergal eri-bàd á-dam-bi ní um-ši-te "Nergal, having terrified their walled cities and habitations, ..." dim-gal-an-ki-a is the *axis mundi*, the world pole that connects the earth and the heavens. It is used to describe both the centrality of the city of Nippur and Enki's home in the abzu: note Išme-Dagan A, line 184: Nibru^{ki} dim-gal-an-ki su-bi ḫu-mu-du$_{10}$-du$_{10}$ "May Nippur, the *axis mundi*, be well off!" and "Enki and the World Order," line 1: é-zu maḫ abzu-ta si$_{9}$-ga dim-gal-an-ki-a "Your house, majestic, placed in the apsu, is the *axis mundi*."

33'. For šu gal-bi du$_{7}$ note "Ninurta's Exploits," line 474: en-me-en á nam-ur-saĝ-ĝá-mu šu gal-bi ḫé-ni-du$_{7}$ "I am the lord. May you exercise my heroic power perfectly," and Samsuiluna C, line 8: me nam-nun-na šu gal-bi ḫé-ni-du$_{7}$ "May you exercise the *me*s of princeship perfectly."

34'. For ḫi-li gú è cf. Inana B, line 154: nin-mu ḫi-li gú è ^{d}inana zà-mí "My lady enveloped in allure, Inana praise!"

35'. We have made the emendation based upon Ibbi-Sîn E, line 12: en me-kù-kù-ug me-sikil šu-luḫ zalag nam [...] "Lord who [determines?] the sacred *me*s, the holy *me*s, the lustrous rites."

36'. For en-ḫuš see our commentary to composition no. 4:1–3.

37'. We have understood mú-mú as a variant for mu$_{4}$-mu$_{4}$ "to be clothed," which makes better sense than mú-mú "to grow." Note CT 17 3:22 (CAD N/1 237 sub *namrirrū*): ní-gal mu$_{4}$-mu$_{4}$ kur-daĝal-la-a si-a "clad in awesome luminosity, filling the wide earth."

39'. For a somewhat similar concept, cf. *kakkabē šamê ina manzāzišunu* GUB-*ma* "the stars of haven stood in their positions (and took the correct path)" (CAD M/1 237b).

40'. This particular syntax with u$_{6}$-di—gub is unattested elsewhere, and so our translation is somewhat tentative.

41'. The intent of this line is not totally clear to us. Alternatively perhaps "Lord to whom the fifty *me*s have given control of the crook and nose-rope," though only one of the *me*s, not all fifty, would seem to be sufficient, since each *me* governed a different function.

42'. It makes little sense for the moon('s crown) to be called a demon, particularly on his greatest day, the day of the full moon. We, therefore, have understood udug to be a variant for udug$_{2}$ "weapon." Note that all three other literary occurrences of udug$_{2}$ occur as udug$_{2}$-maḫ (ETCSL), as would occur in our text. Understanding udug-maḫ as a variant for "great weapon" is logical since it explains why the passage then states that kings bow down. For en-nu-ùĝ zal, note "Nanše and the Birds," line 49: ^{d}ḫa-yà^{mušen} en-nu-ùĝ-ĝá u_4 mi-ni-íb-zal-zal-e "The peacock spends the day keeping watch." For ḫé-e "is indeed," cf., e.g., Išme-Dagan A, line 87: maškim nam-lugal-ĝá ḫé-e "He is indeed the constable of may kingship." If our reading ḫé-e is correct here, then perhaps it occurs only in this passage and not the previous ones following the number of the day because it is the moon's greatest day and ḫé-e is used to emphasize this.

43'. Cf. to our line Sîn-iqīšam A, line 9: ^{d}Nu-muš-da dumu-nun-na mùš me-lem_4 du_8-du_8 "Numušda, princely son, spreading (his) awesome appearance" and for me-lem_4 du_8 note Ur-Namma C, line 7: dub-lá-zu me-lem_4 du_8-du_8-a kur-kur-ra diri-ga "your platform spreading an awesome radiance, surpassing in the lands." But the slightly preserved sign here appears more likely to be šu and not du_8.

44'. For gan "cloud," see most recently Cohen, *Festivals*, p. 252.

It is unclear whether to read ní-gal-bi (awesome splendor) or—in light of the first half of the passage—im gal-bi "at night, the rain greatly (or: the great rain)...."

YBC 4650 obverse

YBC 4650 obverse lines 10' to 20'

YBC 4650 obverse bottom

YBC 4650 reverse

What an astonishing thing a book is. It's a flat object made from a tree with flexible parts on which are imprinted lots of funny dark squiggles. But one glance at it and you're inside the mind of another person, maybe somebody dead for thousands of years.

Carl Sagan

6. When the Moon Fell from the Sky

This intriguing composition, of which only about one third is preserved, involves a plea to Ninlil asking that she intercede in ending the social instability caused by the ominous position of the moon. The lunar phenomenon that most often comes to mind in such a situation is an eclipse, as can be noted by the large number of lunar eclipse omens in the astronomical series "Enūma Anu Enlil" (tablets XV–XXI). There is, however, another foreboding state of the moon: when it is at a negative latitude.

F. Rochberg describes the effect of the moon's latitude as reflected in Mesopotamian omens (Rochberg, *Heavenly Writing*, p. 141):

> If (the moon) sets its face from the middle toward positive latitude, prosperity and greatness... In another horoscope...is the statement "The moon goes from negative latitude toward the node," that is, "with decreasing negative latitude," followed by a line referring to "good fortune" (lit. "propitious days").

For the negative effect of a negative latitude note the omen "If the moon has negative latitude, the economy will perish" (see CAD Š/3 325 *s.v. šuplu* mng. 2).

That the latitude of the moon is the subject of this work may be discerned in several lines. First, the moon is described as passing through ḫar-ra-an-kur-ra, the mountain pass (line 64), finally reaching kur-sig "the base of the mountain" (line 71). Second, the moon is said to touch the earth (line 69). And third, Enki says "(Have) a positive (nim) latitude!" (line 71).

The text is addressed to Ninlil. She is addressed in the second person in line 13: "Oh Ninlil, the tablet of my fate have you erased" and she is mentioned by name four times on the remaining obverse. The reason the speaker invokes Ninlil may be that as the moon's mother she will care for matters involving her son. That may also be the reason she is invoked throughout as "Mother Ninlil."

The host of the Ekur is enumerated, which may reflect some type of rite or activity in the Ekur in reaction to the problem or their joining in the plea that Ninlil take action.

Ninlil, responding to the plea, requests that Damgalnuna ask her husband, Enki, to use his magical powers. Enki then utters an incantation that causes the moon to begin its ascent back to a positive latitude. The last three lines, lines 71–73, could be just the closing narrative. However, line 71, or lines 71–72, or even 71–73 could be the actual incantation uttered by Enki:

71. "(Have) a positive latitude!" The incantation(?)
    In the mountain depths the restorative waters, ... closed above.
72. At his going out, it(?) opened; at his entering, it(?) closed.
73. ... there should be no discord in the land.

The opening words of the first line of our work are no longer preserved, so there is no notation that might indicate that our text itself is an incantation. We hypothesize that these last three lines allude to the following mythological scenario. The moon has fallen to earth, down to the mountain depths, heading all the way down into the *abzu*. There, "the restorative waters" of Enki's *abzu* revitalize the moon, which now begins its ascent back to its rightful place in the heavens. Note that in line 65 Ninlil(?) speaks to Damgalnuna ki-sun$_5$-na "at the entrance." The same term is used when describing the entrance to the abzu in "Ninurta and the Turtle," line 37: ki-sun$_5$-na ká abzu-a, where a door or gate is mentioned. Thus, the references to "opening" and "closing" in line 72 may refer to the gate or entrance to the abzu opening as the moon departs the abzu and then closing behind him as the moon enters the sky.

The structure is as follows:

Lines 1–4	The speaker describes how the discord in the land has affected him personally.
Lines 5–8	The host of the Ekur is listed, possibly indicating activity in the Ekur as a response to the problem or also pleading with Ninil.
Lines 9–?	The breakdown of social order everywhere is described.
Lines 20–21	Ninlil may actually be addressing her son Suen. If so, it is apparently in vain.

Long break

Lines 63–68	Ninlil asks Damgalnuna to ask her husband Enki to help, which Damgalnuna does.
Line 69	The moon reaches its lowest latitude.
Lines 70–73	Enki recites an incantation to cause the moon to begin its ascent, thereby restoring tranquility in the land.

YBC 4658
104×70×27

obv.

1. [x x x (x)]-⸢x x⸣ mè-ka ur$_5$-šè gù mu-un-⸢ra⸣-ra
2. [x x x] ⸢x x zi$^?$⸣ a-uru$_5$-ke$_4$ é-e ì-ug$_5$-ge
3. [x x x x] ⸢á-zi$^?$⸣ [...] du$_6$ saḫar-a tuš ba-GUB
4. [x x x x]-e ⸢x-gi$_4$-gi$_4$$^?$⸣-[(x)] *da-ik* za-e kaš-mu ⸢mùš$^?$⸣ ba-túm
5. [(x) x x x]-a-da ^{d}Nuska sukkal-^{d}En-líl-lá [x x] mu-ra-gub-bu
6. [(x) š]ár-ùr piriĝ ka-du$_8$-a *(x-)x-mu* ^{d}Kal-kal [ì-du$_8$]-⸢é⸣-kur-ra-ke$_4$ uru$_3$ ḫé-ak-e
7. [(x) š]ár-gaz igi nu-túm-mu *la ba-bi-il pa-ni* ^{d}Nin-nisig [ĝiri$_2$-lá-é-kur-ra-ke$_4$ ...]
8. ⸢mi⸣-tum saĝ-50 diĝir-imin [......]
9. ki ad-da-ne-ne gi$_4$-gi$_4$-dè [...]
10. mí-ús-dam-mu šu nam-sa$_6$-ga {ĝeš$^?$.túg}ĝeštug$^{??}$ [...]
11. ^{d}nin-líl-le šu nam-ḫul-a šà-ga-né [...]
12. á-še dam dam-ma-ni-šè inim-ma sa$_6$-ga [n]u-ĝá-ĝá ní-bi [(x)]
13. ^{d}nin-líl-le dub nam-tar-ra-mu šu-zu-šè mu-gur-ra x
14. dumu-zu ki ne-áĝ (*erasure*?) ĝá-⸢a$^?$-ra$^?$⸣ ḫul ⸢x⸣ [...]
15. ì-ne-éš-ta dumu ama-ni ki la-ba-ra-an-[túm]
16. inim ^{d}En-líl-lá-šè ^{d}nin-líl-e ki-a [x]
17. i-gi$_4$-in-zu unu$_2$-tur-ra [x]

tu-ša

18. ama ^{d}nin-líl-le x x [...]
19. sig$_7$-sig$_7$ ĝá-ĝá-da-n[i-šè$^?$ ...]

i-na x x (x)-ki/di-ša

20. ama ^{d}nin-líl-le [...]
21. dumu-ni [...]
22. dumu-mu a-a [...]

23. [š]u mu-d[u$_{7}$ …]

24. [x m]u […]

25. [x] ⸢x⸣ […]

(about 16 lines destroyed)

rev.

(about 4 lines destroyed)

46. ⸢x⸣ […]

47. túg-⸢zi$^{?}$ x⸣ […]

48. ì-du$_{10}$-ga […]

49. ^{d}Dam-gal-[nun-na ...]

50. ki-daĝal ⸢x⸣ […]

51. ama […]

52. ⸢x⸣ […]

(4 lines destroyed)

57. x- ra […]

58. [su]d-rá-áĝ [...]

59. silim-ma ^{d}En-ki [...]

60. ⸢èš⸣-e ZU.[AB-a ...]

61. [x] ^{d}Dam$^{?}$-[…]

62. [ù]-mu-un ^{d}En$^{?}$-k[i$^{?}$ ...]

63. [a]-⸢a⸣ ^{d}EN.ZU-e in-d[i … ^{d}EN.ZU(?)]-⸢e$^{?}$⸣ in-di kur-⸢ra$^{?}$⸣

64. [ḫar]-ra-an-kur-ra-ke$_{4}$ […..] du$_{11}$-ga-na-ab

65. [x-r]a$^{?}$ ki-sun$_{5}$-na-t[a … ^{d}Dam]-gal-nun-na-ra du$_{11}$-ga-[na-ab]

66. [sud]-rá-áĝ x ⸢x⸣ […] DI ⸢x⸣ (x)

67. [x x] kù ^{d}Dam-gal-nun-n[a-k]c$_{4}$ ⸢a-a ^{d}En⸣-ki {ĝeš.túg}ĝeštug-⸢e$^{?}$⸣ ba$^{?}$ ⸢šúm$^{?}$⸣(-x)

68. {x] ⸢x⸣ šul ^{d}EN.ZU ta$^{?}$ [x x x x x] gù mu-un-na-dé-e

69. ^{d}EN.ZU-e šu-ni ki bí-in-tag mu-na-bé ba-da-an-gub

70. ^{d}En-ki šul-⸢^{d}EN.ZU⸣-na-šè inim-ma mu-na-ab-bé

71. [n]im tu$_{6}$ kur sig-ga a ti-la [x x]-bi an-na keše$_{2}$-da

[…] ⸢*ši*$^{?}$*-pa*$^{?}$⸣*-at KUR ša-*⸢*ap*$^{?}$*-x x x x*⸣

bot.

72. è-da-ni-šè ĝál ì-da$_{13}$ ku$_{4}$-da-ni-šè ì$^{?}$-keše$_{2}$-da

73. [...] kur-ra ⌜šà-íb⌝ nu-tuku

[... *uggat lib*]*-bi ul i-šu*

60+10[+] x

TRANSLATION

1. ... of battle therefore screamed out.
2. ... rise(?) and the floodwaters kill at home.
3. ... violence(?) ... sit in tells and dirt ...
4. ... murdered ... you have discontinued(?) my (supply of) beer.
5. ... Nuska, the vizier of Enlil, is at your disposal.
6. May the *šarur*-weapon, a lion with jaws agape, and Kalkal, the doorkeeper of the Ekur, protect you.
7. The merciless *šargaz*-weapon and Ninnisig, the bu[tcher of the Ekur ...],
8. The fifty-headed mace, the Seven Gods ...
9. Restoring the place of their ancestors ...
10. My wife has ... benevolence entirely and,
11. oh Ninlil, ... malevolence in her heart.
12. Now, among themselves, a spouse doesn't speak kindly to the other spouse.
13. Oh Ninlil, the tablet of my fate have you erased.
14. You loved your children, but you hate me.
15. Henceforth, a child doesn't bury his mother.
16. At the order of Enlil, (you?) Ninlil ... in the ground.
17. Perhaps ... a scant meal(?) ...?
18. Mother Ninlil, ...
19. As she sobbed(?) ...
20. Mother Ninlil, ...
21. [called out to(?)] her child ...
22. "My child, father ...
23. ... perfects ...

(About 24 lines destroyed)

47. ... best garment ...
48. ... fine oil ...
49. Damgalnuna ...

50. … the wide earth ...
51. Mother …
(5 lines destroyed)
58. Shining …
59. Well-being ... Enki …
60. At the shrine, in the abzu ...
61. Damgalnuna(?) ...
62. Lord Enki(?) ...
63. He should go/speak to Father Suen ... He should go/speak to Suen at the mountain.
64. Speak … at the mountain pass.
65. ... at the place of entry speak to Damgalnuna …
66. Shining …
67. … Father Enki listened to holy Damgalnuna.
68. … youthful Suen … he/she spoke to him.
69. Suen's hand touched the earth. He (Enki) spoke to him and stood by him.
70. Enki spoke a word to the youthful Suen:
71. "(Have) a positive latitude!" The incantation(?)
In the mountain depths the restorative waters, … closed above.
72. At his going out, it(?) opened; at his entering, it(?) closed.
73. … there should be no discord in the land.

NOTES

1. For a-uru$_5$-ke$_4$ "floodwaters," cf. Proverb Collection 13 no. 34 (Alster, *Proverbs*, I, p. 211): a-uru$_2$-ke$_4$ gù al-dé-dé-e "the flood waters roar."

3. Cf. "Inana's Descent to the Netherworld," line 341: saḫar-a im-da-an-tuš.

4. For gi$_4$ *dâku* "to murder," see CAD D 36. Cf. "Lament for Sumer and Ur," line 311: unu$_2$-gal-bi kurun làl mùš im-ma-ab-túm "wine and syrup ceased to flow in the great dining hall."

5. For gub with the infix -ra- "to place at one's disposal," cf. Dumuzi-Inana P, line 29: ^{d}Inana me-e a-ra ab-gub-bé-en "Inana, I will place them at your disposal."

6–8. The šár-úr, šár-gaz, and the fifty-headed mace were the weapons of Ninurta. for which note "Ninurta's Return to Nippur," lines 129–131:

á-zi-da-mu šár-ùr-mu mu-da-an-ĝál-la-àm
á-gáb-bu-mu šár-gaz-mu mu-da-an-ĝál-la-àm
u$_4$ zú-50-mu mi-tum-an-na-mu mu-da-an-ĝál-la-àm

On my right I have my "Sweeps Away 3600"-weapon; on my left I have my "Kills 3600"-weapon; I have my fifty-toothed storm, my mace of heaven.

6. The lion with jaws agape refers to the *šarur*-weapon and is not a separate entity. For uru$_3$—ak, "to be vigilant," "to stand guard over," note "The Flood Story," line 10: mu níĝ-gilim-ma numun nam-lú-ulu$_3$ uru$_3$ ak "Because of being vigilant over the animals and the seed of mankind."

7. A parallel usage with saĝ instead of igi seems to be our text no. 4:52: udug ḫul-ĝál saĝ nu-túm-mu "merciless evil demon."

9. The term ad-da-ne-ne "forefathers" "ancestors" occurs also in Proverb Collection 1 no. 141 (Alster, *Proverbs*, I, p. 28): é(?) … šeš lipiš-ta ad-ad-ne-ne in-gul-lu-uš "The brothers destroyed their ancestral estate in anger."

10-11. For the contrasting of nam-sa$_9$-ga and nam-ḫul-la elsewhere, note Proverb Collection 2 no. 123 (Alster, *Proverbs,* I, p. 69): nam-sa$_6$-ga kaš-àm nam-ḫul kaskal-àm "The Pleasure—it is the beer! The discomfort—it is the journey." Both lines 10 and 11 have šu, the meaning of which here is unclear. For šu nam-sa$_6$-ga see "The Advice of a Supervisor to a Younger Scribe," line 48: a-šà-za šu nam-sa$_6$-ga ḫé-bí-gi$_4$ "I have restored quality to your fields," and Šulgi X, line 20: šu na-ám-sa$_6$-ga-na-ka "in his fair hands." Could šu here refer to the exercise of power, somewhat similar to Akkadian *qātu*, thus "the exercise of benevolence" and "the exercise of malevolence"?

13. For dub nam-tar-ra, cf. "Ninurta and the Turtle," line 4: dub nam-tar-ra-bi abzu-šè ba-an-gi$_4$ "The tablet of destinies returned to the abzu."

14. Perhaps ki ne-áĝ is for ki ì-ne-áĝ. Cf. "Lugalbanda and the Anzu Bird," line 311: u$_4$-da eri-ni ki ḫa-ba-an-áĝ ĝá-a-ra ḫul ḫa-ba-an-gig "She loves her city, but she hates me."

16. ki-a in this broken line raises the possibility that this line may refer to Enlil ordering Ninlil to take some action regarding the unburied bodies of the mothers in the preceding line.

17. There are two or three very poorly preserved signs in the left margin. See the comment to line 19. The expression unu$_2$ gal "large dining hall" or

17. The expression unu$_2$ gal "large dining hall" or "large meal" is very common (see ETCSL). So perhaps our line, in these times of distress, is expressing the opposite, the absence of plenty.

19. For sig$_7$-sig$_7$ ĝá-ĝá "to sob," cf. S. Maul, *Eršahunga*, p. 208 line 18: ⸢sig$_7$-sig$_7$⸣ nu-ĝá-ĝá *it-ḫu-sa ul ikalla* (CAD N/1 p. 132 *s.v. naḫāsu* B). Note also "An Elegy on the Death of Nannaya," lines 52–53 where sig$_7$-sig$_7$ parallels ér ĝá-ĝá: ér im-ĝá-ĝá-a-ni ér arḫuš [x x]-àm i-im-sig$_7$-sig$_7$-ga-a-ni ki-áĝ šà kù-ga-kam. Most certainly in our text it would make sense for Ninlil to be sobbing over all the misfortune that is besetting the land, as recounted in our text.

20. The scribe has written "10" in the left margin, which presumably marks every tenth line.

47–48. These two lines may refer to Damgalnuna making herself attractive. For a relationship between túg and ì-du$_{10}$-ga note "Debate Between Winter and Summer," line 239: túg ì-du$_{10}$-ge ba-ab-du$_7$-me-en "I perfect the garments with fine oil."

60. The phrase èš-e abzu-a occurs in five other texts (see ETCSL).

62. We do not expect the Emesal form ù-mu-un, but such intrusions do occur, as Ga-ša-an-gal in the hymn to Sîn-iddinam (herein no. 3, line 10).

63. Both di *alāku* and di *qabû* make sense here. The indirect object of the verb "to go" can take the locative. Note, e.g., Inana D, line 52: ^{d}Inana a-a-zu ^{d}Suen-gin$_7$ an-šà-ge àm-gen "Inana, you go into the interior of heaven like your father Suen."

65. For ki-sun$_5$-na referring to the entrance to the abzu in "Ninurta and the Turtle," see our discussion above. For sun$_5$ *erēbu* "enter" see Erimḫuš II 92 (CAD E 259b) and ePSD *s.v.* sun$_5$.

67. To support kù as modifying Damgalnuna and not the term missing at the beginning of the line, note that kù ^{d}Dam-gal-nun-na occurs in four other compositions (see ETCSL). From our interpretation of the context, it is Enki listening to the plea of Damgalnuna to intercede in the matter. Both parties involved in the act conveyed by the phrase {ĝeš.túg}ĝeštug šúm can have -e appended. Cf. "Enki's Journey to Nippur," line 58: é-maḫ ^{d}En-ki-ke$_4$ {ĝeš.túg}ĝeštug kalam-e šúm-mu "The lofty temple of Enki, which bestows wisdom on the land."

69. This line apparently describes the moon reaching its lowest point in regard to earth.

71. The terms nim (*šūqu*) and sig (*šuplu*) respectively denote positive and negative latitudes of the moon (see CAD Š/3 325 *s.v. šuplu* mng. 2).

For kur sig, cf. Enlil A, line 76: kur-sig itima-kù ki ní te-en-te-en-zu "You refresh yourself in the deep underworld, the holy chamber"; Sjöberg, *Temple Hymns,* p. 28 line 187: ki-ul kur-sig galam-e ĝar-ra "Eternal place, deep mountain, founded in an artful fashion."

For ti-la "restorative," see CAD B 311 *s.v. bulṭu* mng. 2.

YBC 4658 obverse

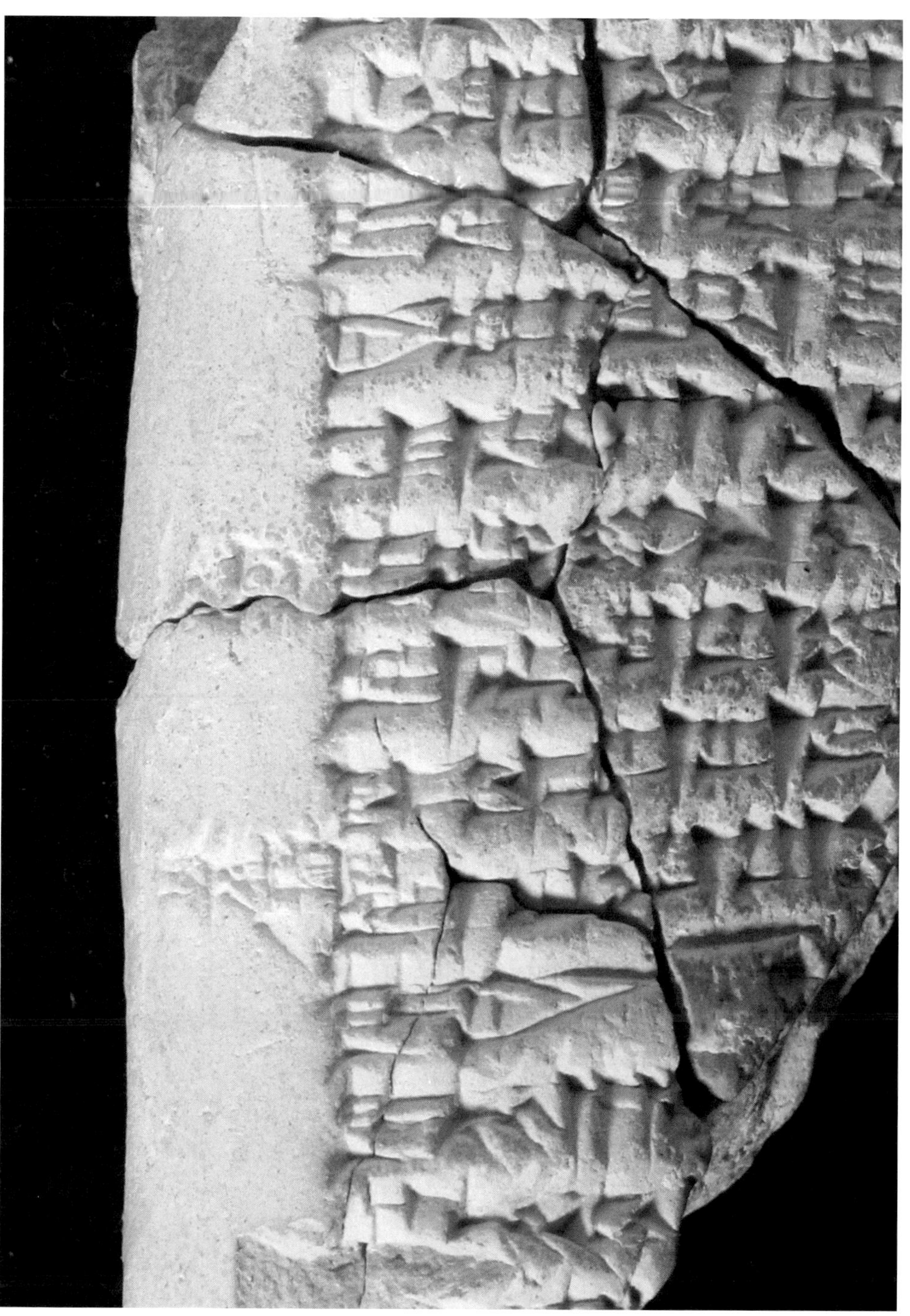

YBC 4658 left edge

YBC 4658 reverse

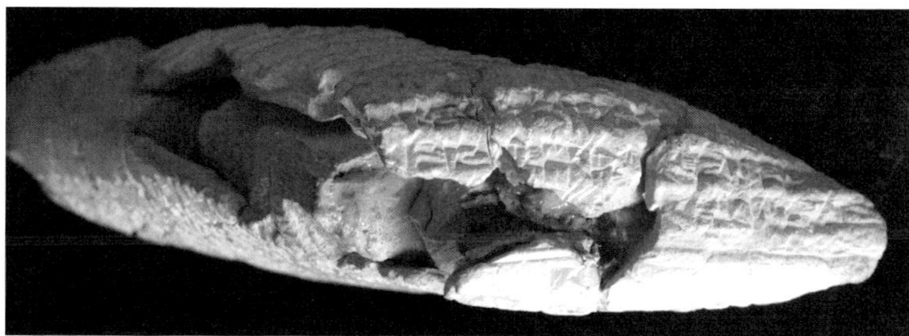

YBC 4658 reverse bottom

Books are the carriers of civilization. Without books, history is silent, literature dumb, science crippled and speculation at a standstill.

Barbara Tuchman

7. A Hymn to Utu Upon the Renovation of a City

This Old Babylonian hymn to Utu may have been recited upon the reconstruction or beautification of a city's walls, as inferred from lines 13 and 14: "its walls made perfect with beauty" and "an adornment of new luxuriance."

The structure is as follows:

1–10	Utu is praised presumably so he will protect the renovation or to acknowledge that the renovation is in Utu's honor.
11	Praise of Šerida, Utu's spouse
12–14	The beauty of the city's wall is described.
15–17	Šerida and Utu are mentioned, and Utu's wisdom is lauded.
18–22	These lines appear to be an added warning to anyone either wishing to do harm to the renovations or perhaps those who would misuse the contents of this tablet.

The opening line of our work parallels the incipit of an Ur III hymn to the goddess Nisaba: nin me {ĝeš.túg}ĝeštug sud an-né ki-áĝ "Lady of the *me* of profound wisdom, beloved by An" (YOS 22 no. 32).

The condition of the text is very poor. Although the tablet itself is only slightly cracked, the surface is badly worn away so that many of the cuneiform wedges are no longer or just partially visible.

YBC 7094
107×67×32

obv.

1. en me {ĝeš.túg}ĝeštug s[ud …]
2. me saĝ-keše$_2$ ⸢ur$_4$-ur$_4$-re⸣
3. di-ku$_5$ šà-ge p[à-d]è ⸢x⸣ [x x x]
4. eš-bar-ra ⸢kíĝ⸣ [x] ⸢x x x⸣ nam ma-tar

5. ulu$_3${lu} zà-du nu-tuk-a ⸢íb$^?$-bi$^?$⸣ du$_{11}$-ga
6. inim-bi nu-sa-sa
7. šul u[r-sa]ĝ ní-gal é-ri-a
8. [x] ⸢x⸣ [x] šu$^?$ na ke$_4$
9. ⸢i⸣-lim u$_4$-ĝál saĝ-ĝi$_6$-ga la-la[(-bi)]
10. un zi ĝál ú a lu-lu nu-laḫ$_4^?$
11. ^{d}Šè-ri$_5$-⸢da⸣ nin-gal ⸢me⸣-ḫuš-a mí zi-dè-eš du$_{11}$-ga
12. ul ḫi-li saĝ-bi guru$_3$
13. eri an-šè sá bàd-bi nam-sa$_6$-ga šu du$_7$-a
14. lum-lum gibil$_4$ ḫé-du$_7$
15. dam-gal ki-áĝ ur-saĝ šul $^{d?}$[Ut]u$^?$ (x)
16. ⸢x⸣ kù-⸢zu⸣ ⸢x x x x x x⸣
17. šà-kúš-ù-bi sud-rá

(large space to the end of the obverse)

rev.

18. [x] ⸢x x⸣ kù$^?$-ga$^?$
19. [x x] ⸢x⸣ maḫ-bi im-sig
20. [x x] ⸢x⸣-ni na-me nu-gub-bu
21. [x x]-da nu-še um-ši-gub-bé saḫar$^?$-ra$^?$ šubtu$_6^!$ ⸢an$^?$ di$^?$ li$^?$⸣
22. šubtu$_6^!$ ḫul-bi ĝar-ra

TRANSLATION

1. Lord of the *me* of profound wisdom ...
2. who cares for and collects the *me*s …
3. Judge, favorite …
4. (who) makes decisions. …, and decides the fates for me.
5. A raging tempest without equal,
6. whose utterances cannot be swept away.
7. The young man, the hero, clad in overpowering light,
8. …
9. Is he not the illuminating radiance, the luxuriance of the black-headed,
10. the provider for the people and all life no matter how numerous they be?

11. and Šerida, the great lady who takes care of the awesome *mes*.
12. Its top bearing joy and delight,
13. The city, which reaches the sky, its walls made perfect with beauty,
14. is an adornment of new luxuriance.
15. The great spouse, the beloved of the hero, the youthful Utu,
16. …
17. whose counsel is profound.

rev.

18. …
19. … the mighty brought low.
20. None can withstand his …
21. For the disobedient who would stand by ... in the dust a trap …
22. Place a horrible trap!

NOTES

2. Cf. to our line the Letter from Sîn-iddinam to Utu, line 9: ur-saĝ dumu ^{d}Nin-gal-e tu-da me saĝ-keše$_2$ ur$_4$-ur$_4$ "Hero, child born by Ningal, who cares for and collects the *mes*" and Ur-Ninurta A, line 73: saĝ keše$_2$ me níĝ-nam-ma mu-un-ur$_4$-ur$_4$ šu-ni-šè mu-u$_8$-ĝar "Caring, he collected the *mes*, whatever there was, and took control of them."

4. For another example of a passage referring to both making decisions and assigning the fates, cf. Nanna F, line 13: eš-bar-ra nam mu-un-di-bi-íb-tar-re.

5. ePSD and the ETCSL read zag-ša$_4$. However, note Sjöberg, *Temple Hymns*, p. 59 commentary to line 44 for zag-du-a-na with variant zag-di-a-na (though one might argue for a reading here zag-sá-a-na). For íb du$_{11}$ cf. "Ninurta's Return to Nippur," line 24: íb du$_{11}$-ga-ni kur ad$_6$ "His angry utterance made a corpse of the mountain."

6. We have understood the verb sa-sa here on the basis of sa-sa = *akāšu* "to move away." Perhaps somewhat analogous to our usage here, note *māmīta ukkušu* "to remove a curse" (CAD A/1 264a). For sa-sa "shining," see Sjöberg, *Mondgott*, p. 128; for "pointed," see ibid. p. 130 n. 3.

7. For ní-gal see CAD N/1 237 *s.v. namrirrū* and said of Utu note 238a: *ša namrirrū bēlūtišu mātāti saḫpū*(?) "Šamaš, whose lordship's awesome splendor overwhelms(?) all the lands."

é-ri-a denotes a wasteland and the epithet "radiance of the wasteland" is possible, though unlikely. Rather, we have understood é-ri-a to be a variant for a-ri-a based on the later bilingual line Angim I 4: ní-ḫuš a-ri-a *ša puluḫtu ezzetu* [*ramû*] (CAD E 434 *s.v. ezzu*).

9. For i-lim u_4-ĝál elsewhere, note the hymn to the moon Nanna L, line 2: i-lim u_4-ĝál ri-a-na íl-la, "rising high as he casts an illuminating radiance."

10. The phrase zi-ĝál un lu-a (with variant zi-ĝál un šár-ra [Ur-Ninurta A, line 20]) occurs in two other literary compositions (Iddin-Dagan A, line 100; "The Exaltation of Inana," line 63). Somewhat similar to our line is Samsu-iluna E, line 18: saĝ-$ĝi_6$ zi-ĝál a-na lu-a ú-a-šè $laḫ_5$-$laḫ_5$-e "Serving as provider for humans and all life, no matter how numerous they be."

12. Cf. to our line Ur-Ninurta A, line 79: ḫi-li ul gùr-ru. Presumably, saĝ-bi in line 12 anticipates eri in the next line.

13. For an-šè sá "to reach the sky," cf. Maqlû II, line 223 (CAD K 274b) *šamāmi ikšudū*. For bàd šu—du_7 as in our line, cf. Ninkasi Hymn, lines 6, 8 (Civil, Beer Goddess): bàd-gal-bi šu mu-ra-an-du_7-du_7 "She finished its great walls for you."

14. Cf. to our line Lipit-Ištar H, line 4: x (x) ḫé-me-a lum-lum $gibil_4$ ḫé-du_7.

16. The first sign might be šà; note šà-kù-zu "your shining heart" in "Man and His God," line 118. kù-zu here could also be "wisdom," which would seem to accord well with the next line.

17. kúš-ù can denote "to be tired, unsettled"; šà kúš-ù is *mitluku* "advice" (CAD M 154a). The latter meaning seems more likely if there is a restoration ⸢šà⸣ kù-zu "wisdom" in the previous line. Alternatively "Its troubles are far away."

18–22. These lines appear to be an added warning to anyone either wishing to do harm to the newly renovated works or who would misuse the contents of this tablet. We base this conclusion on two factors. First, the text itself appears to be a warning, rather than part of the main text, though one could see otherwise. Second, is the large unused space at the end of the obverse. Were these lines part of the main text, we would expect them to be a continuation on the obverse, immediately following line 17.

20. For na-me nu-gub "withstand, "resist," cf. "Ninurta's Exploits," line 570: ^{na_4}ú-ru-tum na-me nu-gub-bu "…-stone, which none can resist."

21. For nu-še, presumably for nu-še-ga, cf. Inana C, line 114: za-e-da nu-me-a nam-nam-ma nu-un-tar sá galam nu-še "Without you no destiny at all is determined, no clever counsel is agreed upon."

The sign šubtu$_6$ is KASKAL+PÚ/PÚ (see CAD Š/3 172b *s.v. šubtu*). Our sign is PAP+PÚ/ PAP+PÚ. Note that the four wedges of the KASKAL sign greatly resemble the four wedges of PAP/PAP and so we believe that our sign is either a writing of the šubtu$_6$ sign or should be considered a variant šubtu$_x$. Also note the Early Dynastic Word List C (M. Civil, CUSAS 12) for the entry PAP.PÚ.BI (p. 223) and PAP.PÚ (p. 224). šubtu$_6$ can denote either a dwelling or an ambush.

an-di-li might perhaps be syllabic for an-dùl "protection," or di-li might be syllabic for dul "to cover" (thus saḫar-ra dul "to cover in dust"). However, there is no other occurrence of syllabic writing in this text.

YBC 7094 obverse

YBC 7094 reverse

Everybody does have a book in them, but in most cases that's where it should stay.

Christopher Hitchens

8. Ninisina's Journey to Nippur

A Complete Old Babylonian Recension

This text, from the private London collection of Mr. Ahmad Saeedi, contains, with but a few breaks, the entire Old Babylonian (OB) recension of the *šir-namšub* "Ninisina's Journey to Nippur." Until now, this *širnamšub* was partially preserved only in a very small OB fragment (CBS 15132) and in two bilingual Middle Assyrian (MA) texts (VAT 9308 [KAR 15] and VAT 9304 [KAR 16]). The colophons to both the OB and MA recensions list the composition as containing 49 verses. The colophon to the MA recension cites the text as a *širnamšub* of Ninisina, whereas the OB cites it as a *širnamšub* of Gula, a goddess who either merged with Ninisina or, by at least the Old Babylonian period, was another name for or aspect of the goddess.

The work first appeared in translation by A. Falkenstein in his *Sumerische und akkadische Hymnen und Gebete*, pp. 68–70. Then, in 1975, I published a transliteration of the text in "Incantation Hymn: Incantation or Hymn?" *Journal of the American Oriental Society*, 95. And, in 2008, a treatment of the OB fragment and the two MA texts, including a copy of CBS 15132 and new copies of the two MA texts, was produced by Klaus Wagensonner, "Nin-Isina(k)s Journey to Nippur: A Bilingual Divine Journey Revisited," *Wiener Zeitschrift für die Kunde des Morgenlandes*, 98, pp. 277–94.

Our new text fills in the many gaps and breaks in the MA version and, in some instances, contains substantive textual differences. We can now know the incipit of the work: nin-gal maḫ-di an-uraš-a, "The great lady, the exalted one of Heaven and Earth." This incipit is unattested in any catalogue, but is somewhat similar to the incipit of "Enki and the World Order": en maḫ-di an ki.

The OB recension is divided into three *kirugu*-sections, whereas the MA recension is written as one continuous composition, without any delineated structural divisions.

Kirugu 1: At daybreak Ninisina leaves her cella in the Egalmaḫ at Isin, while the people offer prayers. She is then paraded through the city to an awaiting boat that will take her to Nippur, all the while accompanied by gods and symbols.

Kirugu 2: The king joins the entourage on the boat to Nippur, which traverses the Kirisig canal in Isin, sails up the Euphrates, and finally moors at the Quay-of-Wine at Nippur. She enters Enlil's temple, the Ekurzagin, where offerings are performed. Enlil then determines Ninisina's fate, that she should continue to reside in Isin, which means that the city of Isin and its king will remain firmly entrenched in power. She then returns to Isin by boat, where, first at the quay, then at the city gate, and finally in all the streets, she is shown great honor. The populace spends the night in merry-making, celebrating the successful outcome of Ninisina's journey.

Kirugu 3: Ninisina and her spouse Pabilsag perform the marriage ritual to ensure a good year, which has begun propitiously with the trip to Nippur and the decreeing of a good fate. The two then proceed to the throne room. Offerings are made and the king offers up an ox and sheep. Music is played and the gala-priests officiate, including invoking the chief deities of the pantheon. Lastly, libations are performed by the king.

The scribe of our text identifies himself in the colophon as Ibbi-Sîn. Although most of the text is in standard Sumerian, in a few cases Ibbi-Sîn employs unexpected variants (e.g., šà for ša_4) or syllabic writings (e.g., gu-ru-un for kurun). In one case he even conflates two syllabic orthographies in the same word: ú-lu-šin-ši-en for ulušin "beer." He also, in some instances, adds a pronunciation gloss in smaller script below the line. But perhaps the most unexpected aspect of Ibbi-Sîn's ductus is his total omission of the NE sign, which he either forgot how to write—which is hard to believe—or purposely avoided, perhaps playfully, just as some modern essayists occasionally take up the challenge of writing short compositions that omit a particular letter of the alphabet. Nowhere does the NE sign occur and in the instances where it should, Ibbi-Sîn has substituted variants:

Line 2: ga-àm-mi-i-DE-en for ga-àm-mi-i-DÈ-en

Line 18: BI-in-nu-ús for BÍ-in-nu-ús

Line 20: PI-in-du for BÍ-in-du

Line 41: mi-ni-ib-gul-gul-NI for mi-ni-ib-gul-gul-(e-)NE
and possibly Line 47: -NI-a for -NE-a

Our OB text provides a glimpse into the evolutionary process by which a Sumerian work was tradited through centuries. The fact that the natural language of the scribes was not Sumerian only exacerbated the process, a process that could involve not only copying from another tablet, but writing from dictation or memory, a methodology easily open to error. One should keep in mind that our copy of the OB recension does not appear to be the work of a "master scribe." Variants in the MA recension may have originated in a different OB recension, such as CBS 15132, and thus may not always be MA-period variants.

Below we have included only the Sumerian text of the bilingual MA recension. However, where we believe it to be significant, we have commented upon the MA Akkadian text in our notes. For a thorough presentation of the Akkadian rendering we refer you to Wagensonner's above-cited edition in *Wiener Zeitschrift*.

Saeedi 0212
125 × 95

obv.

1. nin-gal maḫ-di an uraš-a
   MA: [ga]l maḫ-d[i] an ^{d}Uraš-[
2. kù ^{d}Nin-ì-si-in^{ki}-na dumu-an-na me-tés̆ ga-àm-mi-i-de-en
   MA: [ ]-in-si-an-na [ ] me-téš ḫé-i-[
3. é-ta ḫúl-la-a-ni nam-ta-è u$_4$ é-agrun-na-⸢x⸣
   MA: ⸢é⸣-ta ḫúl-la-ni nam-ta-è u$_4$ é-agrun-na-⸢x⸣
4. kalam-ma-ni ^{d}Utu-è-dè šùd mu-un-na-an-šà
   MA: kalam-ma-ni ^{d}Utu-è-gin$_7$ silim-ma mu-na-ŠA$_4$
5. sila-daĝal eri-na-ka mi-ni-[di]b-bé eri-ni mu-un-da-sá
   MA: sila-daĝal eri-na-ke$_4$ mi-ni-in-dib-bé eri-ni mu-un-da-sá
6. nitlam-a-ni ur-sag̑ $^{[d]}$Pa-bil-sag̑ ḫi-li-a mu-da-an-DU
   MA: nitlam-a-ni ur-sag̑ ^{d}Pa-bil-sag̑ ḫi-li-a mu-un-DU
7. dumu ki-ág̑-g̑á-ni ^{d}Da-mu sa$_6$-ga munus-zi ^{d}Gu-nu-ra
   MA: dumu ki-ág̑-g̑á-ni ^{d}Da-mu sa$_6$-ga nu-nus-zi ^{d}Gu-nu-ra
8. ^{d}Lama$_2$-sa$_6$-ga é-gal-maḫ-a-ke$_4$ eg̑ir-ra-né im-mu-ús
   MA: ^{d}Alad-sa$_6$-ga é-gal-maḫ-a-né eg̑ir-ra-na mu-un-su$_8$-ge-eš

9. ^{d}Alad-sa$_6$-ga a-a-ni $^{[d]}$En-líl-e zi-da-né mu-un-DU
   MA: ^{d}Udug-sa$_6$-ga a-a $^{]}$En-líl-lá zi-da-na mu-un-DU

10. ^{d}Udug-sa$_6$-ga en ^{d}Nu-nam-nir-ra gùb-bu-né mu-un-zi
   MA: ^{d}Lama$_2$-sa$_6$-ga en ^{d}Nun-nam-nir-ra gùb-bu-na mu-un-DU

11. šu-nir-ra-ni zalag an-na-ke$_4$ [i]gi-ni-šè si im-sá
   MA: ^{d}šu-nir-ra-a-ni zalag-an-na-gin$_7$ igi-a-ni-šè si mi-ni-íb-si

12. šu-maḫ sukkal-zi é-gal-maḫ-a-ke$_4$ igi-šè mu-un-⸢na⸣-DU
   MA: ^{d}šu-maḫ sukkal-zi é-gal-maḫ-a igi-šè mu-un-DU

13. e-sír sila-daĝal mu-un-na-ab-sikil-e eri mu-un-na-ab-kù-ge
   MA: e-sír sila-daĝal mu-un-na-ab-sikil-e eri mu-un-na-ab-kù-ge

14. èš Nibru^{ki} dur-an-ki-a-šè saĝ-íl-la mu-un-DU
   MA: èš Nibru^{ki} dur-an-ki-⸢a⸣-šè saĝ-íl-la mu-un-[DU]

---

ki-ru-gú 1 ⸢kam⸣-ma-àm

---

15. ⸢íd⸣kir$_{11}$-sig-e ^{ĝeš}má mu-da-ri lugal mu-un-da-ab-le-e
   CBS 15132: luga]l mu-u[n-
   MA: íd ^{id}kir$_{11}$-sig-a mu-un-da-ab-ri ⸢lugal⸣ mu-un-na-ab$^{?}$-bal$^{?}$

16. lugal-e gú-tab$^{!!}$ min-na-bi ĝiri$_3$ mu-un-na-ĝá-ĝá
   CBS 15132:] ⸢x x min$^{?}$-na⸣-bi ĝiri$_3$ mu-na-[
   MA: lugal-e gú-tab min-a-bi ĝiri$_3$ mu-na-ĝá-[ĝá]

17. ^{id}Buranun-na uz^{mušen}-kù-gin$_7$ mu-un-da-ab-diri ^{d}EN.<LÍL>^{ki} mu-un-da-ḫúl
   CBS 15132: ^{id}Buranun-na uz-kù-⸢ge⸣ mu-un-na-diri [
   MA: ^{id}Buranun-na$^{!}$ gi-úš-kù-⸢ge⸣ mu-un-na-diri Nibru^{ki} mu ⸢un⸣-d[a-ḫúl]

18. kar-ĝeštin-na-ke$_4$ ^{ĝeš}má bi-in-nu-ús Nibru^{ki} mu-un-da-ḫúl
   CBS 15132: kar-ĝeštin-na-⸢ka⸣ má bí-in-ús ^{d}EN.L[ÍL^{ki}]
   MA: kar-ĝeštin-na-ke$_4$ má bí-in-ús ^{d}EN.<LÍL>^{ki} mu-un-da-ḫ[úl]

19. sun$_5$-na-ni é-^{d}En-líl-lá-šè àm-ma-da-an-ku$_4$-ku$_4$
   CBS 15132: sun$_5$-na-⸢ni⸣ é-^{d}En-líl-lá-šè àm-m[a
   MA: sun$_5$-na-ni é-^{d}En-líl-lá-šè àm-ma-da-an-ku$_4$-[ku$_4$]

20. é-[ku]r-za-gìn-^{d}En-líl-lá-ka nindaba sa pi-in-du
   CBS 15132: z]a-⸢gìn⸣-$^{[d]}$En-líl-lá-ke$_4$ nindaba sá b[í-
   MA: é-kur-za-gìn é-^{d}En-líl-lá-ke$_4$ nindaba sá bí-in-[

21. kisal-[daĝa]l-la kisal-^{d}En-líl-lá-ka gu$_4$ udu mi-ni-ib-šár-šár
    CBS 15132:]-^{d}En-líl-lá-ka gu$_4$ udu mi-n[i-
    MA: [kisa]l-maḫ-e kisal-^{d}En-líl-lá-ke$_4$ gu$_4$ udu mi-ni-[

22. lugal-e KI.LUGAL.GUB u$_4$-sud-ra-ka šu mu-ni-mu-mu
    CBS 15132: GU]B u$_4$-sud-rá-ka šu mu-n[i-
    MA: [lug]al-e ki-lugal-gub u$_4$-sud-rá-ke$_4$ šu mu-ni-mu-mu

23. ^{d}En-líl-le saĝ-ki-⸢zalag$_2$⸣-ga-a-ni mu-un-šè-zi-zi
    CBS 15132: -k]i-zalag$_2$-ga-ni mu-un-[
    MA: [^{d}E]n-líl-le saĝ-ki-⸢zalag$_2$⸣-ga-a-ni mu-un-š[i-

24. ^{d}Nin-líl-le igi [ḫú]l-ḫúl-a-ni mu-un-šè-bar-bar-re
    CBS 15132:]-ḫúl-la-ni ⸢x⸣ [
    MA: [^{d}Ni]n-líl-le ḫúl-ḫúl-a-ni mu-un-š[i-

25. ^{d}Nin-ì-si-in[^{ki}-n]a dumu-an-na-ra nam mu-ni-ib-tar-re
    MA:]-⸢x⸣-na dumu-an-na nam ⸢x⸣-[

26. eri-zu ki-tuš ki-á[ĝ]$^{?}$ ḫé-re-dím ki ge-en ḫa-ra-ab-[ĝar]
    MA:] ⸢x⸣ ge-en ki-en-gi [

rev.

27. ⸢x (x) lugal⸣ [u$_4$ ...]-⸢x⸣-zal-la-re
    MA: u$_4$ m]u-un-di-ni-í[b-zal-...]

28. íd-maḫ-e é DIĜIR [ ] ⸢x⸣ nam-ta-è

29. íd-da a-ḫúl-la ⸢x⸣ [^{id}Bura]nun-na-kam mu-un-zal

30. kar-kù eri-na-ka [kala]m$^{?}$-⸢ma$^{?}$⸣-né mu-un-da-ḫúl

31. abul e eri-na-ka imin-bi ĝál mu-un-na-da$_{13}$-da$_{13}$ da-da

32. sila-daĝal eri-na-ka giri$_{17}$-zal-e ki mu-un-na-ni-ib-tag

33. sila ì-si-in^{ki}-na-ka giri$_{17}$-zal-e ki mu-un-na-ni-ib-tag

34. kalam-ma-ni asila$_3$ ĝi$_6$ zal-la-ri šu mu-un-na-ab-du$_7$ du

---

ki-ru-gú 2-kam-ma-àm

---

35. i-lu ama$_5$-ni-šè ama$_5$-ni-šè

36. é-La-ra-ak^{ki}-a me en ki-áĝ-ĝá-ni saĝ íl-la mu-un-DU

37. nitlam-a-ni ur-saĝ ^{d}Pa-bil-saĝ gaba nam-ma-da-ri
    MA:] ur-saĝ ^{d}Pa-[

38. šu-un-ni-a šu im-ma-an-du ḫúl-ḫúl-e im-šà
    MA:]-a šu im-ma-an-dab$_5$ [

39. gú-un-ni-a gu$_4$-da im-da-lá mí-du-ge-eš mu-un-né
   MA: [g]ú-ni gú-da im-ma-an-[

40. é-gal-maḫ ama$_5$-ki-áĝ-ĝá-ni-šè àm-⸢ma⸣-da-an-ku$_4$-ku$_4$
   MA: é-gal-maḫ ama$_5$-ki-áĝ-a-ni-šè à[m-

41. bara$_2$-gal-maḫ-bi dúr$_{\text{du-ur}}$-bi mi-ni-ĝar-re-éš ⸢níĝ$^{?}$⸣ mi-ni-ib-gul-gul-né
   MA: bara$_2$-gal-maḫ-ba dúr$^{!}$ mi-ni-in-ĝar-re-éš níĝ mi-[

42. balaĝ-kù-ki-áĝ-ĝá-ni nin-ḫe-nun ^{d}Nin-igi-zi-bar-ra
   MA: balaĝ-kù-ki-áĝ-ĝá-ni ^{d}nin-ḫe-nun-n[a

43. šìr-kù zà-me-en lá $_{a}$-la ĝál-la-ni gu-<<ḫé>>nun-di ì-ku$^{?}$-re<-eš>
   MA: šìr-kù zà-mí la-la ĝá-la-ni gù-nun mi-ni-[

44. ub-kù balaĝ-kù-ga šu-uš mu-un-na-ta-ke$_4$
   MA: ^{kuš}ub-kù balaĝ-kù-ge šu mu-⸢un⸣-tag

45. gala ri-a mu-un-na-zi-zi-zi ^{d}Nin-ì-si-in^{ki}-na-ra
   CBS 15132: r]i-a m[u-
   MA: gala ri-a mu-un-na-zi-zi e-ne-ra ^{d}Nin-in-si-[

46. an ^{d}En-líl ^{d}En-ki ^{d}NIN-maḫ-bi mu-un-na$^{?}$-ḫun-ĝá-ta
   CBS 15132: ^{d}E]n-líl ^{d}E[n-ki
   MA: an ^{d}En-líl ^{d}En-ki ^{d}NIN-maḫ-e mu-un-ḫun-ĝá-e-da

47. $^{<<d>>}$nin-maḫ-e é-gal-maḫ-an-ni-a ki-tuš mi-ni-in-du$_{10}$-ga-ta
   CBS 15132: -ma]ḫ$^{?}$-⸢e⸣ [
   MA: $^{<<d>>}$nin-maḫ-e é-gal-maḫ ne-a ki-tuš mi-ni-íb-du$_{10}$-ga-ta

48. lugal-e gu$_4$ mu-un-na-ab-gaz-e udu mu-un-na-ab-šár-e
   MA: lugal-e gu$_4$ mu-un-na-ab-gaz-e udu mu-un-na-ab-šár-re

49. làl ĝeštin ú-lu-šin-ši-en gu-ru-un [ka]š-maḫ mu-un-na-ba-ab-le-e
   MA: làl ^{ĝeš}ĝeštin kaš-zíz-sù kaš-sù mu-un-na-ab-bal-bal-e

---

ki-ru-gú 3-kam-ma-àm

---

dub 49 mu-bi-im
šìr-nam-šu-ub-^{d}Gu-la-kam
   MA: šìr-nam-šub-^{d}Nin-in-si-na-ke$_4$
im-gíd-da I-bi-^{d}EN.ZU

TRANSLATION

1–2. Let me praise the great lady, the exalted one of Heaven and Earth, holy Ninisina, the offspring of Heaven.

3. In her joy, she leaves the temple at (first) light at(?) (her) *kummu*-cella.

4. Her nation, at sunrise, utters a prayer to her.

5. She traverses the public square of her city and her city accompanies her.

6. Her husband, the hero Pabilsag, in full virility goes (with her).

7–8. Her beloved son, Damu the Handsome One, and the faithful woman Gunura—they are friendly guardians of the Egalmaḫ—follow behind her.

9. A friendly spirit—he is her father Enlil—goes at her right.

10. A friendly genie—he is the lord Nunamnir—goes up at her left.

11. Her standard—it is the gleaming one of heaven—goes straight in front of her.

12. Šumaḫ—he is the faithful vizier of the Egalmaḫ—goes at the front

13. and cleans the streets and the public square for her; he purifies the city for her.

14. (The procession) proudly goes to the shrine Nippur, the axis of heaven and earth.

It is the first *kirugu*.

---

15. She directed the boat along the Kirsig-canal and the king crosses over.

16. The king steps on both banks.

17. It floats in the Euphrates like a glistening duck and Nippur rejoices.

18. She moored the boat at the Quay-of-Wine and Nippur rejoices.

19. Reverently she enters into the temple of Enlil.

20. At the Ekurzagin of Enlil she arranged for offerings.

21. In the [broad] courtyard, the courtyard of Enlil, she slaughters oxen and sheep.

22. The king in the ancient King's Stand prays.

23. Enlil raises his gleaming countenance to her.

24. Ninlil looks at her full of joy.

25. For Ninisina, the child of Heaven, he there determines (her) fate:
26. "May your city be made for you a beloved dwelling place! May it [become] for you a permanent place!"
27. After the king ... has spent the day ... [in joy?] ...,
28. at the grand canal ... departs.
29. In the canal the joyous waters ... of the [Euphra]tes flow.
30. At the shining quay of her city ... her [natio]n(?) rejoices at her.
31. The gates of her city, all of them, open wide for her.
32. In the public square of her city (the city) makes obeisance to her.
33. In the streets of her city (the city) makes obeisance to her.
34. Her nation, after spending the night rejoicing, does everything perfectly for her.

It is the second *kirugu*.

---

35. (To) the song "To her cella! To her cella!"
36. —it is(?) the Elarak—her beloved lord(?) goes there confidently.
37. Her husband, the hero Pabilsag, met her.
38. He took her in his arms and made joyous sounds.
39. They embraced and spoke tenderly to each other.
40. They enter the Egalmaḫ, her beloved cella,
41. and take their seats on the grand, august dais. Provisions are provided in great quantity.

42–43. Her beloved sacred harps, Ninḫenun and Ninigizibara, enter(?), resounding in sacred song and rapturous praise.

44. The sacred drum and sacred harp play for her.
45. The gala-priests side-by-side(?) rise for her, for Ninisina.
46. After An, Enlil, Enki, and NINmaḫ have soothed her,
47. after the great lady in her Egalmaḫ has made (her) dwelling pleasant,
48. the king slays an ox for her, slaughters a sheep for her,
49. and libates honey, wine, emmer-beer, *k*-beer, and first-quality beer for her.

It is the third *kirugu*.

The tablet has 49 verses.
It is a *širnamšub* of Gula.
The tablet of Ibbi-Sîn

NOTES

4. The MA -gin$_7$ instead of the OB -dè may result from our Akkadian-speaking scribe using Sumerian gin$_7$ as he would the Akkadian conjunction *kīma*, "when," "as soon as."

The MA has silim-ma mu-na-DU *ina šulme illak*. However, the OB indicates that DU was originally read ša$_4$.

7–12. The OB and MA texts vary in lines 7–10. The OB has the order: Lama, Alad, Udug, whereas the MA has Alad, Udug, Lama, although both recensions agree as to the order of gods listed.

Falkenstein understood Alad, Udug, Lama as being separate participants in the procession, whereas Wagensonner understands ^{d}Lama$_2$-sa$_6$-ga é-gal-maḫ-a as referring to the role of Damu and Gunura in the procession, the second ^{d}Lama$_2$-sa$_6$-ga to be the father of Enlil (though it is "father Enlil"), and ^{d}Udug-sa$_6$-ga to be Nunamnir(ra). In the OB recension each of these lines is constructed as PN$_1$ PN$_2$-e + intrans. verb. -e here would seem to be the demonstrative particle suggested by Edzard, *Sumerian Grammar* 7.3. If so, then Wagensonner's understanding is the correct one, for, if so, PN$_2$ modifies or identifies PN$_1$. Moreover, note our composition no. 3, lines 15–16, wherein Nanna is called the ^{d}Lama$_2$-sa$_6$-ga of Sîn-iddinam.

8. The similarity of the sounds /us/ and /su/ may indicate that an error possibly from dictation may be at least partially responsible for the MA variant.

10. The implication of the verb zi rather than the expected du, as in the previous line and as in the MA, is unclear to us.

15. The Kirsig or Mirsig canal ran through Isin. We have restored the verb as ri based on the MA recension, where the scribe translated *irḫuṣ* "washed" in a context that had by then omitted má and had thus lost its original sense. má ri is "to direct a boat." Cf., e.g., Ur-Namma C, line 105: ... kar-za-gìn-na ^{d}Nanna-ka má na-an-ga-mu-ni-in-ri "I have directed ships to ... and the lapis-lazuli quay of Nanna."

17. The MA metaphor is a far-less attractive gi-úš-kù-ge diri "drifting holy(?) dead reeds." This error may have resulted at some point from a confusion

of the sounds /uz/ and /uš/ during dictation. Note also that the MUŠEN and GI signs are not that dissimilar, so the source of the error might be a little more complicated—after all, Ninisina's boat was made of dead reeds. The MA scribe translated *udittu*, a kind of reed, Sumerian gi-ḫenbur$_{(2)}$, rather than the perhaps expected *uššu*, Sumerian gi-úš, "dead reed." Interestingly, in CT 13 37:25 we find the two terms juxtaposed: gi-úš gi-ḫenbur$_2$ (CAD U 308 *s.v. uššu* B).

18. We suggest that an error in transmission of this line has occurred by the MA period. At some point the sign LÍL in ^{d}EN.LÍL.KI was omitted and so the MA translator read it as ^{d}En-ki, translating ^{d}*É-a*, a god out of place for Nippur. Wagensonner offers a different solution (p. 289): "The OB manuscript C [CBS 15132] mentions instead of Enki Nippur which leads to the conclusion that the content was slightly adapted by adding ^{d}en-ki mu-un-da-ḫ[ul$_2$]."

19. sun$_5$-na ku$_4$ "to enter humbly" occurs also in Ur-Namma C, line 199: sun$_5$-na-bi mu-un-ku$_4$; and Ur-Ninurta A, line 13: sun$_5$-na-bi mi-ni-in-ku$_4$. The MA translation of sun$_5$-na-ni is the expected *ašriš*, "humbly." However, we wonder if the expression sun$_5$-na ku$_4$ is an intentional word play, since a plural form of the verb ku$_4$ is sun$_5$ and ki-sun$_5$-na (as in no. 6, line 65) means "entrance way."

    Note that the exact same phrase é-^{d}En-líl-lá-šè àm-ma-da-an-ku$_4$-ku$_4$ occurs in "Ninurta's Return to Nippur," line 101.

20. sa pi-in-du is syllabic for sá bí-in-du$_{11}$ "to arrive."

21. The MA recension has kisal-maḫ-e instead of kisal-[daĝa]l-la.

22. The MA renders KI.LUGAL.GUB as *šubat bēlūtišu*. For the reading of KI.LUGAL.GUB with a final /l/ note Ur-Namma C, line 13: lugal KI.LUGAL.GUB-la ḫé-du$_7$-bi kisal-maḫ-e si-a "The king, the ornament of ..., occupies the august courtyard." However, also note "Lament for Sumer and Ur," line 435: KI.LUGAL.GUB-bu-na nidaba ba-kúr "the food offerings at his ... were altered" and "Uruk Lament," line 14: KI.LUGAL.GUB-ba.

23. A similar line occurs in Šulgi X, line 80: šul ^{d}Utu saĝ-ki zalag-ga-ni mu-ši-ib-zi-zi. Note also Išme-Dagan A+V, line 104: saĝ-ki zalag-ga-ni ĝá-a-šè ḫu-mu-ši-in-zi.

26. In the MA text ge-en ki-en-gi appears to have evolved from dím(=gin$_7$) ki ge-en in the OB. Wagensonner, not having our OB recension at his

disposal, restores the broken Akkadian line as KUR *li*[*p-ri*(?)-*ik*(?)], noting in his commentary "gi/gin$_6$ has an Akkadian equation *parāku*, 'to block oppose'." Wagensonner's restoration seems contrary to the intent of the original OB, where the Sumerian verb to be restored was assuredly positive in tone.

27. The MA verbal form, based upon our OB text, can now be restored. For several occurrences of the form u$_4$ mu-un-di-ni-ib-zal-e, see the ETCSL.

31. This line is similar to a curse in a Sumerian law code: [abu]l eri-na-ke$_4$ ⸢ĝál⸣ [x]-tag-tag "May the gates of his city be wide open!" P. Michalowski and C.B.F. Walker, "A New Sumerian 'Law Code'," *Studies Sjöberg*, p. 388 iii 16'. The form abul-e eri-na-ka is most unexpected. It may be an error caused by the sound of the next word eri. Another possibility is an error in placing the locative marker. Note that the object being opened can sometimes take the locative, "Enki and Ninḫursag," line 172: ^{d}Uttu šà-ḫúl-la-ni-ta é-e ĝál ba-an-taka$_4$ "Joyfully Uttu opened the house."

32. For ki—tag denoting an act of obeisance, note Inana C, line 5: inim-maḫ-a-ni-šè ^{d}a-nun-na-ke$_4$-ne kušum$_4$ ki mu-un-tag-ge-ne "The Anuna gods kowtow before her august word."

35. Though i-lu often denotes a lament, it can also denote a joyful song, for which note, e.g., Nanna B, line 59: ^{d}Nanna-mu i-lu-zu zé-ba-àm i-lu šà-ab-ĝá-kam "My Nanna, your chant is sweet; it is the chant of my heart." Most certainly the repetitive "ama$_5$-ni-šè ama$_5$-ni-šè" sounds like a refrain or the beginning of a hymn that was sung as the goddess was taken to her cella.

36. Our extremely tentative translation assumes that -a me en is a sandhi writing for -àm en. Otherwise, the meaning of me(-)en is difficult to discern here. For me-en as syllabic for men "crown" in an otherwise non-syllabic text, note "A Hymn to Inana" (c.4.07.a), line 4: me-en-kù -an-na saĝ-ĝá ĝál-la-e "the holy crown of An placed on her head." saĝ-íl in our text might support this interpretation, thus "in the Elarak she went wearing her beloved crown." However, I am unaware of ki-áĝ elsewhere modifying either men or aga. Moreover, the expression saĝ-íl-la DU "to go confidently" occurs elsewhere (see ETCSL) having nothing to do with the wearing of something on the head. For a passage that relates Ninisina's "beloved" with the "lord" Pabilsaĝ as we suggest in our line, note Ninisina F, line 5: nitalam$_3$ ki-áĝ-ĝá-ni en ^{d}Pa-bil$_2$-saĝ-ĝá.

37–39. These three lines parallel Inana-Dumuzi H lines 6–8:

ù-mu-un ku-li an-na gaba mu-un-ri
ù-mu-un-e šu-ni-a šu im-ma-an-dù (*iḫ-zi-in-ni*)
^{d}ušumgal-an-na gú-ĝá-a gú-da ba-an-lá (*ki-ša-di i-di-ir*)

The lord, the friend of An, met me.
The lord took me in his hands.
Ušumgalanna embraced me about the neck.

The MA has šu—dab$_5$ instead of šu—du, with translation *iṣ-bat*.

Note "Ninurta's Exploits," line 217: ḫúl-ḫúl-le i-im-DU. We assume that in our text šà is a variant for ša$_4$, which is the DU sign.

41. Cf. Šulgi R, line 47 "barag-kù-bi dúr im-mi-in-ĝá-re-éš níĝ mi-ni-íb-gu-ul-gu-ul-ne "They take their seats on its holy dais and provisions are lavishly prepared" and Iddin-Dagan A, line 102: gu$_7$ naĝ gal-gal-e níĝ mi-ni-ib-gu-ul-gu-ul-lu-ne "plentifully provide food and drink."

42. According to AN : *Anum* V 187 Nin-ḫé-nun-na was a bull-lyre of Gula (Litke, *A Reconstruction*, p. 185). Nin-igi-zi-bar-ra was also a bull-lyre, but according to AN : *Anum* IV 73 (Litke, *A Reconstruction*, p. 153), a bull-lyre of Inana. Note Ibbi-Sîn year date 21: mu ... ^{d}Nin-igi-zi-bar-ra balaĝ ^{d}Inana-ra mu-na-dím.

43. Line 43 is clearly corrupt and thus the MA may more accurately reflect the original text. The sign ḪÉ is a result of dittography with line 42. za-me-en instead of zà-me is unexpected. So too is the orthography lá-la, particularly with the gloss a, which, if a pronunciation gloss, would seem to be unnecessary. zà-mí, besides "praise," can be *summû* "lyre," and thus we wonder if somehow the gloss indicates a variant á-la "drum," but this is not reflected in the MA. We are unaware of any other references of la-la ĝál.

The MA verbal form is gù-nun—x (Wagensonner suggests a likely gù-nun—e and so reads the MA translation of the verb as *i-*⌜*da-bu-bu*?⌝).

44. šu-uš may be for šu-šu "two hands," indicating that two instruments are being played together.

45. The MA presumably understands ri-a as ér-ra *taqribtu* (which makes good sense when referring to the gala-priest, as here). However, there is no attestation of the phrase ér(-ra) zi. ri-a here may denote "side-by-side" (see CAD E 254 *s.v. erâ*).

The MA renders Ninisina as Ninkarrak.

46. For the reading of the name ^{d}NIN-maḫ, see our comment to our text no. 5 line 23'. The MA has -e instead of -bi.

47. The MA Akkadian translation *rubātu ṣirtu* for ^{d}nin-maḫ is probably the correct interpretation, since it is Ninisina—not NINmaḫ—whose temple is the Egalmaḫ. Presumably the writing ^{d}nin-maḫ was a mistake resulting from ^{d}NIN maḫ in the previous line. Wagensonner observes that the MA may have noted something strange here in the Sumerian "The Sumerian line starts with an illegible sign which is the divine determinative written over the beginning of the sign NIN. This is forasmuch noteworthy because the translator rendered the DN literally..." (p. 290).

49. For *kurunnu* juxtaposed with kaš-maḫ see CAD K 290 *s.v. kašmāḫu*. The MA Akkadian translation is: *dišpa karāna ulušenna kurunna unaqqāši*. About the forms kaš-zíz-sù kaš-sù, Wagensonner (p. 290) states "The lexicography of kaš-ziz$_2$-su$_3$ with Akk. *ulušennu* is to my knowledge only attested here. We would expect ... KAŠ.ZIZ$_2$.AN. Perhaps this writing was caused by the following kaš-su$_3$ equated with *kurunnu*."

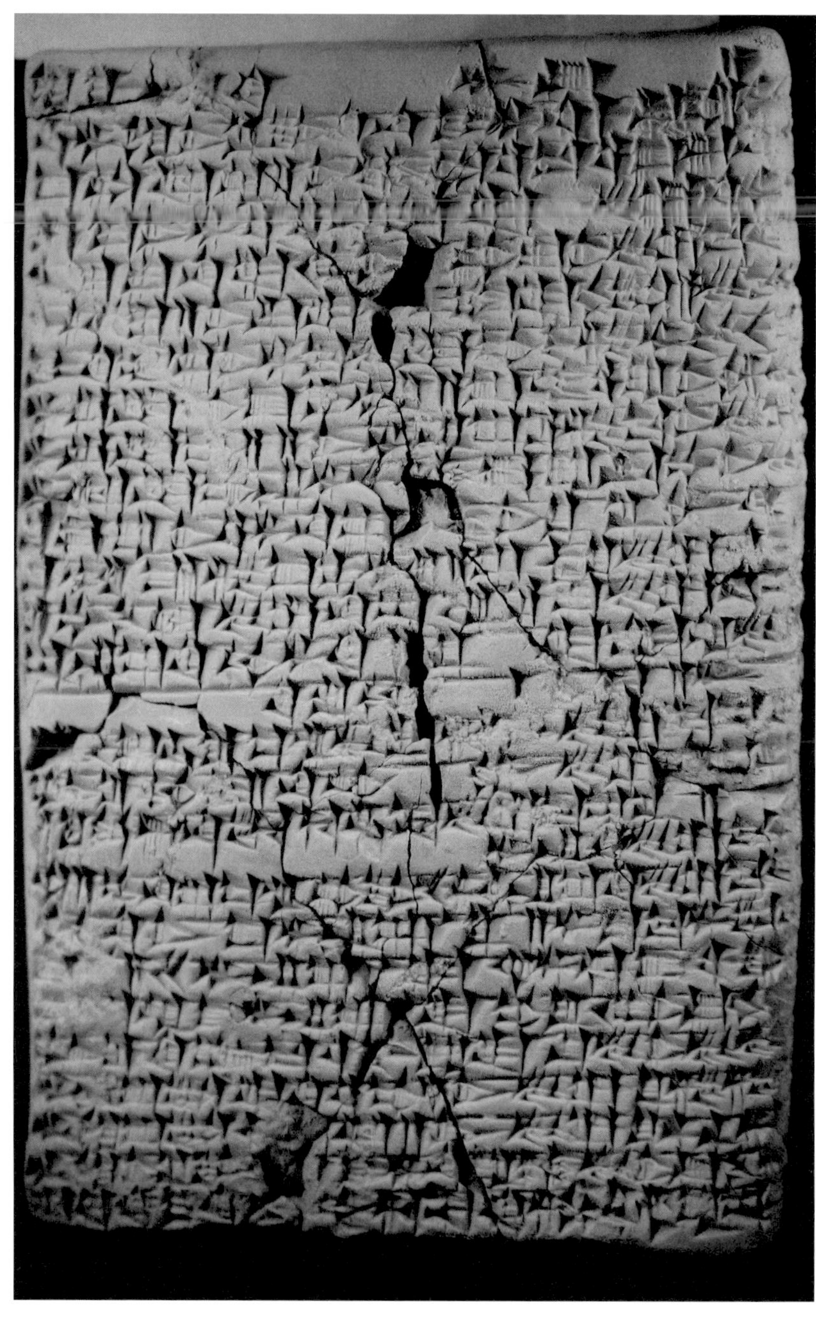

Saeedi 0212 obverse

Saeedi 0212 reverse

Saeedi 0212 reverse

Saeedi 0212 right side

The sole substitute for an experience which we have not ourselves lived through is art and literature.

Aleksandr Solzhenitsyn

9. Tears of a Fallen King

Although he is unidentified by name or title within the text, we suggest that the figure around whom this work is centered is a defeated king who sees himself as the luckless Dumuzi. In the literary narratives, Dumuzi changes form to escape his pursuers, as our poet alludes to by using in our opening line the same words as in the Dumuzi text, $ulutim_2$ bal "to change form" (or, for our king, a change of circumstances). The recurring term ĝuruš in the ensuing refrain is another sign of the king's identification with the lad Dumuzi.

The literary figure who is the speaker of the composition never identifies himself. We speculate that he is a king, for in lines 8–9 he laments the ineffectiveness of his weapon of war, the chariot, in line 7 perhaps the lack of troops or messengers on the roads, and in lines 14–15 he laments that he will be forgotten by history. The Ur III kings and later monarchs saw themselves as Dumuzi, the shepherd of his people. The events described in this text suggest that the king had been defeated and was facing ruin at home. This work, rather than reflecting a real historical situation, may just be scribal speculation as to a king's reaction to defeat.

The author has structurally divided the composition into three parts according to three refrains involving tears or laments (ér):

I.	Lines 2–7	er id me-a	The tears are a river!
II.	Lines 8–18	er mu-ri ti na-a	Tears pour out; there is no end.
III.	Lines 19–26	er mu-ši-ma-ma	Because of this, he will set up a lament.

The composition can be divided on the basis of content.

Lines 2–6: The king bewails his plight, likening his situation to that of the ill-fated lad Dumuzi.

Lines 7–9: The king is defenseless. The roads are dangerous; his chariots and ships are afraid to set out.

Lines 10–13: The world has been turned upside down. Inhabitants of the city leave for the wilderness, to live in less civilized areas. Those who should not be in the city, perhaps referring to country folk without the skills needed for city life, or others hostile to city dwellers, or even enemies and criminals, now enter freely.

Lines 14–15: The king realizes that he has forfeited his place in history as a great man and that he and his descendants will be forgotten. He bewails the fact that even his inscriptions will be of no avail in this regard.

Lines 17–26(?): The king describes how defeat has devastated his kingdom. His city has been burned down. The brickwork has crumbled and is covered with debris. The fields and orchards are ruined.

The text is partially syllabic, which, as we have suggested in the preface, is an indication that our scribe was a novice, as, for instance, can be seen in his continuing of lines around the edge of the tablet onto the reverse, rather than folding long lines on the same side, as was standard scribal practice in southern Mesopotamia.

NBC 7306
164×84×33

1.	[ú-lu]-ti-im ba-la-mu ⸢x⸣ [...]	
2.	[a gu-r]u-uš a-ma-ar-gi [x x] ⸢zi$^{?}$-da$^{?}$ e$^{?}$⸣ gi	er id me-a
3.	[a gu-r]u-uš ba-la ú èn-šè ⸢a⸣-ra-zu	er id me-a
4.	[a gu-r]u-uš èn-bi mu-n[i-tar] [x x]	er id me-a
5.	⸢a⸣ [g]u-ru-uš èn-bi mu-⸢ni-tar ⸣ [x x]	er id me-a
6.	⸢a⸣ [gu-r]u-uš ⸢ba$^{?}$⸣-la sa-ba-ar ⸢e$^{?}$⸣	er id me-a
7.	[x x ḫar$^{?}$]-⸢ra$^{?}$⸣-an i-lim-ma ⸢ri⸣	er id me-a
8.	[x gi-ĝì]r šu-la-mu i-lim-⸢ma⸣ ri	er mu-ri tìl na-a
9.	[x (x) m]á-gi-lu-mu-šè ⸢i-lim⸣-m[a r]i	er mu-ri tìl na-a
10.	⸢AN$^{?}$⸣ [x x mu]-ge-en ú mu-DU	er mu-ri tìl na-a
11.	ú mu-mu-šè mu-ge-en ku-ru$^{!}$ ad dub ni gi-ru-ú	er mu-ri tìl na-a
12.	ú-ru-a nu-di-ti-en i-ni-ku-ra	er mu-ri$^{!(TI)}$ tìl na-a

13.	saĝ-gi-ga nu-⌜dí⌝-ti-en i-ni-ku-ra	er mu-<ri> tìl na-a
14.	mu-da dub-mu-la ⌜sa-re⌝	[er m]u-ri tìl na-a
15.	mu li-la-a-mu a-pa ⌜x⌝	er mu-ri tìl na-a
16.	⌜da$^{?}$-ga$^{?}$-mu$^{?}$(x) da$^{?}$⌝ [x x x x]-⌜gi$_{4}$$^{?}$-gi$_{4}$$^{?}$⌝ KA$^{?}$ da la-a	<er> mu-r[i] <tìl na-a>
17.	di-da-la ⌜mu-mu⌝ la ⌜x⌝ da	er mu-ri tìl na-a
18.	e-mu lu-⌜izi$^{?}$-da$^{?}$⌝ mi-[x x]	er mu-ri tìl na-a
19.	šeg$_{12}$ la-la-bi mi-in$^{?}$-lu$^{?}$-lu$^{?}$ èn-šè i-ni-im ti-le	er mu-ši-ma-ma
20.	i-lu-bi-šè ú mu-mu na-da-mu-ú	er mu-ši-ma-ma
21.	⌜x x x⌝ mu-mu gi-da na-an-da-mu	er mu-ši-ma-ma
22.	[ḫa]-la-ma-da ĝeš la-a na-an-da-mu	er mu-ši-ma-ma
23.	[...]-⌜šè⌝ ⌜še$^{?}$ saḫar-ra na⌝-an-da-mu	er mu-[ši]-ma-ma
24.	[...] ú ⌜gana$_{2}$$^{?}$⌝ na-a[n]-da-mu	er mu-ši-ma-ma
25.	[...] ⌜ú⌝ a mi ⌜x⌝ [x] (x) ma-mu	[er mu-ši]-ma-ma
26.	[... m]i ⌜x⌝ mi-ni-[...]	er mu-ši-[ma-ma]
27.	[...] ⌜x x x x x⌝ [...]	

TRANSLATION

1. My changing condition (lit. "form")! ...
2. Oh the young man ... freedom.
   The tears are a river!
3. Oh the young man who has changed! How long must there be supplication?
   The tears are a river!
4. Oh the young man, the one inquired after ...!
   The tears are a river!
5. Oh the young man, the one inquired after ...!
   The tears are a river!
6. Oh the young man who has changed! ... a net!
   The tears are a river!
7. ... [high]way(?) is beset by deathly silence.
   The tears are a river!
8. My trusty chariot is beset by deathly silence.
   Tears pour out; there is no end.

9. At … my *magilu*-ship is beset by deathly silence.
   Tears pour out; there is no end.
10. … go out …vegetation ….
   Tears pour out; there is no end.
11. Some go out to where the vegetation grows, corpses heaped in piles(?), everyone fearful all the time.
   Tears pour out; there is no end.
12. In the city, those who should not be going about have entered.
   Tears pour out; there is no end.
13. The people who should not be going about have entered. ….
   Tears pour out; there is no end.
14. (Despite) (my) name being recorded on inscribed tablets,
   Tears pour out; there is no end.
15. My name and descendants …
   Tears pour out; there is no end.
16. My dwelling(s) … killed(?) ….
   Tears pour out; there is no end.
17. Glowing embers …
   Tears pour out; there is no end.
18. My house [founded] by the righteous(?)!
   Tears pour out; there is no end.
19. The brickwork in all its splendor is covered(?) over. How much longer until there is closure?
   Because of this, he will set up a lament.
20. At its wail the growing plants no longer grow….
   Because of this, he will set up a lament.
21. … the tall growth no longer grows.
   Because of this, he will set up a lament.
22. At the destruction, the spreading trees no longer grow.
   Because of this, he will set up a lament.
23. At … barley(?) doesn't grow in the dust.
   Because of this, he will set up a lament.

24. … plants no longer grow (in) the field.
Because of this, he will set up a lament.

25. … grows for me.
Because of this, he will set up a lament.

26. …
Because of this, he will set up a lament.

NOTES

1. For ulutim$_2$ bal "to change form" said of Dumuzi, note "Dumuzi and Ĝeštinana," line 34: šu-ni mu-ni-in-kúr-kúr ulutim$_2$-ma-ni mu-ni-in-bal-bal "He changed his hands, he altered his appearance."

2–6. The refrain "a ĝuruš," referring to Damu, occurs also in the opening kirugu of the balaĝ-lamentation eden-na ú-saĝ-ĝá-ke$_4$.

3. For u$_4$ èn-šè note "The Lament for Nippur," line 36: u$_4$ en-šè ì-šub; line 195: íb-si u$_4$ èn-šè ér gul-la e-ne e-ra-an-du$_{11}$-ga.

4–5. The TAR sign is very faint, but visible in line 5. The term èn-bi is attested in literature only with the verb tar (see ETCSL). Presumably the difference between the two lines was the two broken signs. Otherwise the same line would be intentionally repeated—possible but unexpected.

7–9. We have translated the verb ri on the basis of ri *nadû* "to imbue."

8–18. We understand na-a to be for nu-a "there is not." Cf., e.g., Proverb Collection 2 no. 43 (Alster, *Proverbs,* I, p. 53): dub-sar šu nu-a nar milla$_2$ nu-a "A scribe without a hand, a singer without a voice."

8. Our translation "trusty," "reliable" is based upon šu—lá *qâpu* "to trust."

11. We suggest a syllabic rendering of guru$_7$ ad$_6$ dub, "corpses are piled in heaps." The sign we have read ru$^!$ is clearly poorly written, no matter what the actual sign is.

12–13. For di-di *alāku* cf. SBH p. 101 r. 10 (CAD A/1 301): a-sig-ta di-di *ša šapliš illaku* "he who goes about humbly" and AMT 102: 11 (ibid., p. 302): igi-bi-e silim-ma di-di-da *maḫaršunu šalmiš italluki* "to go about well protected in their presence." The form nu-di-ti-en is quite unusual. Based on context the term would seem to describe undesirables who have now entered the city. Perhaps the novice scribe's nu-di-ti-en was for a dictated nu-di-di-e-ne (-e-ne i-ni- > -en i-ni-). nu-di-di here might be serving as a substantive in a plural form, "those who should not be going about." di-di can also mean *qabû* "to speak" (see CAD Q 22), which, if here, would conjure up the English term "unspeakables."

14. For dub-mul-la "tablet with writing," cf. Gudea A v, 23: dub-mul du_{10}-ga bí-ĝál-la-a and "Debate Between Copper and Silver," line 19: ĝeš-šudum-ma dub-mul kù-ta pà-dè. The imagery compares the stars on the heavenly background to the cuneiform signs on a tablet. It is also possible that the term alludes to more than simple writing, but to texts such as hemerologies, astrologies, the secrets of the gods, etc. This line may refer either to the king's own inscriptions or to astrological etc. works that foretold his future. In either case, they are of no use now. mu here has the sense "name" or "reputation."

15. We have understood li-la-a here for li-li-a "descendants." For a somewhat similar context with mu "name" and "descendants" cf. 4R 12 r. 31f. (CAD N/1 259 *s.v. nannabu*): e-ne mu-ni numun-a-ni $isimu_2$-bi im-ri-a-bi ù li-li-a-bi ka un-lu-a-bi ugu a-ba-ni-in-dé "May (Enlil) cause him, his name, his descendants, his offspring, his family, his progeny to disappear from mention by all the multitudes of people!"

One possibility is to interpret a-pa-[šè] as a variant for a-ga-šè, "in the future" (see PSD A/1 69 *s.v.* a-ga mng. 1.3), which in Emesal is a-ba-šè and makes good sense in our albeit broken context, though we hardly expect an Emesal variant here. Note the Emesal Gašan-gal intruding in the non-Emesal Sîn-iddinam hymn herein and perhaps ù-mu-un in "When the Moon fell from the Sky," line 62. Cf. also C. Wilcke, "Sumerian: What We Know and What We Want to Know," (from paper delivered at 53e RAI, 2007) p.12 for the interchange of a-ba and a-ga "rear" in Old Sumerian at Lagaš. Another possibility is to understand a-pa-[šè] as syllabic for an-pa-šè *ana elât šamê*, "to the very heights of heaven," that is to say, everywhere; cf. to our passage VAB 4 120 iii 52 (CAD E 79 *s.v. elâtu*): *ištu* AN.ÚR *adi* AN.PA *ēma* [d]*Šamaš aṣû aj iši nakirī* "May I have no enemies from the base of heaven to the heights of heaven, wherever the sun rises." Lastly, since the line mentions "descendants," we cannot totally dismiss a-pa as a rendering of ab-ba "father."

17. We have interpreted the beginning of the line as dè-dal mul-mul-la "glowing embers."

18. We have understand e mu lu as being for é-mu lú. A line that is peculiarly similar to our line is the "Ur Lament," line 121: é lú zi-dè ba-ab-ĝar-ra-mu "My house founded by the righteous." We suggest that this was the original dictated line and that our novice scribe mangled it by writing the IZI sign instead of the ZI sign. In this line the king is lamenting the fact that even the homes of the best people have not been spared, though this could also be a reference to his own home, the palace.
19. We have interpreted lu-lu as syllabic for lù-lù, which is equated to the N-stem of *katāmu* "to be covered" in MSL 9 p. 96 206: [lù]-lù = *i-ta-ak-tu-mu*. Presumably inim-tìl is for inim-til = *kušurrā'u* "compensation," "closing statement" (see C. Wilcke, *Early ANE Law* 76; referenced by ePSD). Most certainly the much over-used word "closure" seems appropriate here.
23. For the expression še saḫar(-ra) "barley in the dust" cf. Proverb Collection 7 no. 75 (Alster, *Proverbs,* I, p. 161 and ETCSL c6107.B.7.49.58): še saḫar-ba im-ma-an-tìl-la "the barley has been lying in the dirt"; Šulgi B 50 and Šulgi D 346: še-saḫar-ra-gin_7.
24. The sign might well be $gana_2$, which makes sense here, but the dearth of bi-syllabic signs on the tablet gives us pause.

NBC 7306 obverse

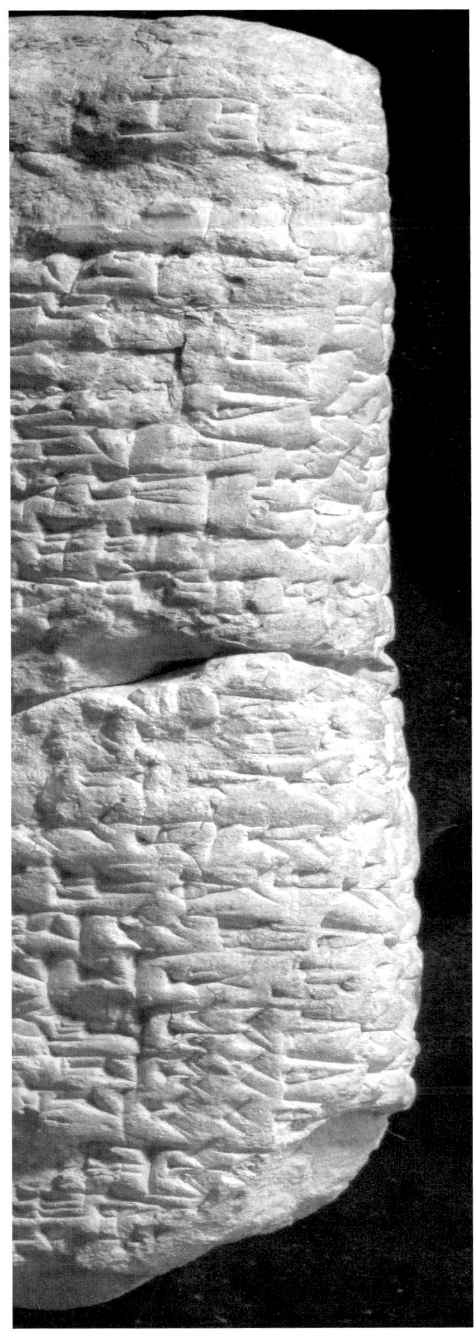

NBC 7306 right edge

NBC 7306 reverse

NBC 7306 right edge and reverse

Literature is the one place in any society where, within the secrecy of our own heads, we can hear voices talking about everything in every possible way.

Salman Rushdie

Index

The main entry is the Sumerian term in the standard form, either non-syllabic or without an unusual variant. The syllabic form or variant as actually appears in the text is given in parentheses after the main term.

ad$_6$	(ad)	9:11
agrun		8:3
ak(-ak★)		1:11'; 4:57★(?); 5:36'
al du$_{11}$		3:19
ama		5:22'; 6:15, 18, 51
ama-ar-g̃i	(a-ma-ar-g̃i)	9:2
ama$_5$		8:35, 40
amaš		4:3
an		5:20', 24', 26', 28', 29', 37', 39', 40', 46'; 6:71; 8:2, 25, 46; 7:13
an-daĝal-la		5:46'
an-gal		2:7
an-ki		1:24'; 2:4; 3:5, 7, 15; 4:1, 44; 5:29', 32', 42', 49'
an kù-ga		5:30'
an-sà-ga		5:47'
an-ta		4:45
an-uraš-a		8:1
asil$_3$(-lá★)		5:10'★; 8:34

—— B ——

babbar		3:20
bàd		5:32'; 7:13
bala	(ba-le, ba-ab-le★, ba-la$^+$)	8:15, 49★; 9:1$^+$, 3$^+$
balaĝ-kù		8:42, 44
bar-ra		3:34
bara$_2$		4:39; 5:12'
bara$_2$-gal-maḫ		8:41
bara$_2$-maḫ		1:31'; 4:24
bàr-bàr		4:2
búr		3:41
buru$_{14}$		3:5, 7

— D —

gú è		5:34'
gú-tab		8:16
gù dé		1:35'; 6:68
gù-nun di	(gu-nun di)	8:43
gù ra-ra		6:1
gu_4		8:21, 48
gub		2:8–10; 3:9; 4:6, 20, 60; 5:12'(?), 39'; 6:3, 5, 69; 7:20, 21;
gùb		8:10
gudug		2:13
$guru_3$	(gi-ru-ú★)	5:9';7:12; 9:11★
$guru_7$	(ku-ru)	9:11
gurum		5:42'

—— Ĝ ——

ĝá-a-ra		6:14
ĝá-ĝá	(ma-ma★)	9:19–26★; 6:12, 19; 8:16
ĝá-nun		4:7
ĝál		2:12, 14, 16, 18; 4:8, 10, 23, 28; 8:31, 43
ĝál da_{13}(-da_{13}★)		4:50★; 6:72; 8:31★
ĝar(-ĝar★); gá-re+		1:26'; 2:10, 11; 3:6★, 13, 18, 21, 23★, 27★, 31; 4:15, 39(?); 5:13'; 7:11, 22; 9:18; 8: 26, 41, 43+
ĝen	(ge-en)	9:10, 11
ĝeš-búr		5:41'
ĝeš-$eškiri_2$		5:41'
ĝeš lá-a	(ĝeš la-a)	9:22
ĝeš-nu_{11}		5:39'
ĝeš-nu_{11} gal		5:21', 26', 28'
ĝeštin		8:18, 49
ĝeštug ĝar		2:10
$ĝeštug_2$		6:10(?); 7:1
$ĝeštug_2$ šúm		2:19; 6:67
$ĝi_6$-a		5:44'
$ĝi_6$ zal		8:34
ĝešĝidri		1:32'
ĝìr		3:42

—— I ——

kù-sig$_{17}$	(kù-zi-ge)	3:12
kù-zu		7:16
ku$_4$	(ku)	8:42; 9:13
ku$_4$-ku$_4$	(ku-ku★)	1:12'★; 5:5', 47'; 8:19
kur(-kur★)		1:23'; 2:5; 4:38★, 55, 56; 5:7'★, 43', 44'; 6:2, 63, 64
kur-sig-ga		6:71
kurun	(gu-ru-un)	8:49
kúš-ù		4:49

—— L ——

la-la	(lá-la★)	7:9; 9:19; 8:36, 43★
lá-a	(la-a)	9:22
lab (la-bi)		1:10'
laḫ$_4$		7:10
làl		8:49
li-li-a	(li-la-a)	9:15
lipiš		2:8
lu(-lu★)		2:12; 7:10★; 9:19★
lú		1:15'; 2:13; 4:9, 48
lú-kúr-ra		4:48
lú sa$_6$-ga		1:28'
lú-zi-da	(lu-izi-da)	9:18
lú-ulu$_3$		2:10
lugal		1:4, 34'(?); 3:1, 15, 26–28, 32, 33, 45; 4:38, 53; 5:42'; 8:15, 16, 22, 27
lugal an-ki-a		1:24'; 3:15
lugal diĝir-re-e-ne		1:31'
lugal kur-kur-ra		4:38
lum-lum		4:5; 7:14

—— M ——

$^{\hat{g}eš}$má		8:15, 18
má-gi$_4$-lum	(má-gi-lu)	9:9
maḫ		1:1, 13', 23'; 2:4, 8, 9; 3:17; 4:4, 7, 17, 24, 44; 5:42'; 8:41, 47
maḫ-bi		7:19

—N—

—— P ——

—— R ——

—— S ——

saĝ nu-túm-mu (cf. igi nu-túm-mu)		4:52
saĝ šúm		4:62
saḫar		6:3; 9:23
sar	(sa-re)	9:14
si		1:21'
si-ĝar		3:24
si-il		5:6', 48'
si sá		8:11
si-sá-eš		3:41
sì-ga		4:16
sig		4:5; 6:71; 7:19
sig$_7$		4:4, 8; 5:27'
sig$_7$-sig$_7$ ĝá-ĝá		6:19
sikil	(si-ki-le★, si-ik-la$^+$)	1:21'★, 31'$^+$; 3:11; 4:43; 5:11', 35'; 8:13
sila		8:33
sila-daĝal		8:5, 13, 32
silim		6:59, 63
silim e		3:44; 5:49'
sipa šà-ga		4:12
siškur$_2$		3:11
su$_8$		4:25
sud-ra	(rá★)	2:5★; 8:22; 7:1, 17★
sud-rá-áĝ		6:58, 66
sukkal		
sukkal-^{d}En-líl-lá		6:5
sukkal-zi		8:12
sun$_5$ (enter)		6:65
sun$_5$ (humble)		8:19

—— Š ——

šà		2:7, 13; 3:13, 24; 4:6, 12, 29, 30; 5:6', 34'
šà dab$_5$		5:11'
šà-ge pà-dè		7:3
šà-ḫúl	(šà ḫu-ul)	1:19'; 3:19, 42; 4:26
šà-kúš-ù		7:17
ša$_4$	(šà)	8:4, 38
šár(-šár★)		8:21★, 48

—Z—

Akkadian

Deities

Royal Names

Temples

Geographic Locations